Earthly Pleasures
and
Heavenly Treasures

Earthly Pleasures

And

Heavenly Treasures

Poems by

CHARLES C. MYERS

Library of Congress Catalog Card Number 89–040635

ISBN: 0–923568–05–0

The collaboration of Fern Harris as artistic consultant
is gratefully acknowledged.

PUBLISHED BY

Wilderness Adventure Books
320 Garden Lane
Box 968
Fowlerville, Michigan 48836

Manufactured in the United States of America

This book is dedicated to the memory of my wife, Mary Lauretta.

The poems contained in this book are expressly for your enjoyment, no de-meaning is intended.

They cover a wide range of subjects, such as:

Miscellaneous
People
Special Occasions
Philosophy
Nature
Fantasy

I wish to express my gratitude for:

- The encouragement of those desiring to have my poems published.

- Those who helped prepare the poems for publication.

- The cooperation and patience of the illustrator.

- The publication and distribution of the book.

- The opportunity to use local talent.

Contents

Miscellaneous

Poems

Writing poems comes naturally—
The ideas and words just come to me.
They seem to come from everywhere
So I assume they come from up there.

God must be helping me in His own way
So I will know just what I should say.
I rearrange them for meter and rhyme
And this is easy most of the time.

Poems are like children, they must have care
And the writer, too, must be made aware.
They need a good start to send them on their way
And a good ending so people will say—

"They're great!"

Poetry — A Form of Art

Poetry is painting with pen and ink
and is just as beautiful, I think.
Beauty, of course, is in the mind
For each is always one of a kind.

A line that is written with a pen
Is like stroking a brush now and then.
Our canvas is paper when we write.
The words we use will give it sight.

If you listen real hard you may hear
The waves of the ocean loud and clear,
Or see the color in plants and trees
As they are swaying in the breeze.

The colors are blended by description
Or mixed together by prescription.
Painting and writing are much the same.
It's just calling them by their right name.

It's true not everyone has agreed
With paintings they see or poems they read.
It's the thought the artist tries to convey
That each one does in their own way.

Music — Another Form of Art

Music is another beautiful form of art
That comes solely from the composer's heart
The mind will always be willing to obey
The things the composer's heart has to say.

Music is divided into three sections—
Composer, conductor, musician selections.
The conductor must choose how he wants them to play
To get the effect the composer tries to convey.

Combining instrumental sounds of melody
With rhythm, timbre, accent and harmony,
in sequence, solo or simultaneously,
The conductor must decide which one it will be.

Music must be emotionally expressive
To both stimulate and to be suggestive,
To stir the listener with laughter or tears
So they will remember it all through the years.

Poems and Bouquets

Poems are like arranging flowers.
Words keep running through your mind
So you have to sort them out
To make them easier to find.

Arranging them in order
So they'll have meter and rhyme
Is something that must be done
Repeating lines time after time.

The same is true with a bouquet.
They must be arranged one by one
Till all the flowers have been used
And the bouquet is finally done.

Now there will be something else
That you must also have to do.
The words must be given meaning
Before your poem will be through.

It must convey a message
That will help someone somewhere,
And show to those who read it
That someone does really care.

The bouquet that you have made
Must express your feelings too,
And bring someone happiness.
That's what you made it to do.

The Sampler

I had almost forgotten, so I chose in haste.
The Sampler seemed right for they have good taste.
The box is so pretty—especially the cover.
It makes a good gift to send to your lover.

Inside the cover it shows their position.
Each one is separate and in good condition.
This arrangement is good for it makes it real handy
For one to select the right piece of candy.

Is it one that is nutty or one that is sweet?
Either one would be real good to eat.
Now the box is all empty, there's no more to choose.
There are so many things for which you can use.

The box, it's too pretty to just throw away,
So keep it and maybe you'll use it some day
For hankies or jewelery or trinkets to store,
Remembering what it was given you for.

A gift from a friend who likes you a lot.
Not just the gift, but mostly the thought.

Delicate Things

There are many delicate things,
Like the beautiful butterfly wings
And the webs that spiders spin
To catch the insects that fly in.

The nests the ants make will all be gone
When they're washed away or stepped upon.
The fireflies that shine their light
As soon as there's darkness of the night.

The hummingbird gathering its food,
The bees making honey that tastes so good,
The scent from flowers we like so much,
And their petals so soft to the touch.

From the delicate pansy to the mums
Will all fade away when winter comes.
The flame that comes from the candle's light
Will go out when you pinch it tight.

The aroma from a fine perfume
As it travels across the room,
The ice cubes put into a drink
Will melt much faster than you think.

A pencil with a point so fine
Could break when we write a line.
The delicate fineness of those with skill
Who can do whatever they will.

The tender clasping of the hand
Shows more feeling than mere words can.
A whisper in somebody's ear
meant just for only them to hear.

A glance across the room at one
Could mean a friendship has begun.

Your New Home

Does the magic spell still ring a bell
And hold you spellbound too?
Take your breath away and then you say
It couldn't happen to you?

You're all aglow and wouldn't you know
There is nothing you can do.
Chills run up your spine, and though you feel fine
The feeling is something new.

Your friends drop in and some of your kin
Then you bid them all adieu.
The thrill of it just seems to fit.
It happens to just a few.

You want to smile and cry a while
It's all in your point of view.
Your first new home to call your own,
And it's made just for you two.

In the Service

The bugler sounds reveile to them all
And they are quick to heed its call
To the first assembly of the day
When their name is called they must say,

"Here" or "Yo." Something so they'll know
They are there and ready to go.
There'll be more assemblies every day
To hear what the sergeant has to say.

They must stand and salute the flag
Even though they can hardly drag.
They must come to full attention
Or they might draw a detention.

To dig a hole, then fill it up
Or dig a ditch with just their cup,
They might have them run a mile
With full gear on them all the while.

They're foolish things to do you say
But they are done so they'll obey.
It's all done by regulation
So they'll get more dedication.

They exercise till they're all in
And then they say now let's begin.
When they're dismissed they go to mess.
The food's not all that bad I guess.

They find time to write a letter
So folks will know that things are better.
The maneuvers are very real.
It takes awhile to get the feel.

Backpacks with everything and more,
Miles of hiking till they are sore,
Live fire flying over their head,
They keep it down or they are dead.

Then there's the foxholes that they dig
Or they will wind up in the brig.
It's all done by regulation
And must have verification.

Now is the time when taps is played.
They wish that it could be delayed
For they're too tired to go to sleep
Or have a date they'd like to keep.

They must go through this most every day.
But it's routine so it is O.K.
In the service of the U.S.A.

Cooking on the Range

The cook stocks the chuckwagon
When cowboys start their drive.
He makes sure they have enough
So they will all survive.

He's cooking for the cowboys.
He serves them one by one.
No matter what he serves them,
They eat it then they run.

On a drive there's not much time
And the biscuits do seem hard.
They soak them in their coffee
And feed them to their "pard"

The spuds are too brown
And the eggs need turning.
The oatmeal is cooking
As he keeps things from burning.

At noon he serves them stew
Along with sourdough bread.
They eat most all of it,
But that's the meal they dread.

Supper time is best of all,
For they get salad and meat.
And the thing that they like most
They get all they can eat.

There's the midnight coffee break.
They come in two by two.
They sip their coffee by the fire
And munch a small snack too.

Cowboys are sentimental folks.
You wonder if that is true.
They are serious on the job.
They're the best at what they do.

They'll sing some songs while sitting
Around the old campfire.
Some will go back to the herd,
The rest of them will retire.

Ranch Life

It was a sprawling ranch with an open range,
And in the early days nothing seemed to change.
It took a lot of people just to run the place.
I don't recall their names but I recall their face.

I remember a guest house being on the place.
It was always ready for guests just in case.
They had built the main house way up on the hill.
It was beside an old tree that is standing still.

It was there a long time before they had arrived.
No telling just how long that old tree had survived.
We used to climb the roots up around and through.
That is the way the roots on that old tree grew.

Papa didn't like us climbing on that old tree.
His method of correction was across his knee.
When new neighbors came to settle on the land,
Papa and some others would lend a helping hand.

To help them get started and get settled in,
Then that is when all the trouble would begin.
They would start to argue over the open range.
Each would claim more than their share and they wouldn't
    change.

Then they would argue over the water rights.
This more than anything would often start their fights.
The more settlers that came the worse it would get.
Now range wars have started and they're not over yet.

Some were beginning to build barbed wire fences.
Other ranchers sought to bring them to their senses.
They were in a frenzy—the worst we ever saw.
This was all happening because there was no law.

Now it was affecting women and children too.
There just had to be something that they could do.
So they called a meeting for all to attend
To see if there was some way all of this could end.

They decided to start a town of their own,
Then work together instead of each alone.
Officials were elected from the people there
That is the only way that it would be fair.

Now each rancher had a place to go to complain
Where it could be resolved and set straight again.
You want to know the name? They called it Riverview.
Like the old ranch, it overlooks the river, too.

Others are coming in, the town is growing fast.
Time healed many wounds, we've almost forgot the past.
Now things are nearly the way they were before.
Of course we can't predict what the future holds in store.

The Variety Store

They started a business on a shoestring.
The shoestring made the register ring,
So they added pencils, notebooks and such,
Being careful not to add too much.

But the customers kept coming back,
So they added glassware and knickknacks.
More and more customers were coming
and the business was really humming.

So a candy counter was added too,
Up in front where it was in full view.
Then lingerie and other women's needs,
Jewelry of all kinds and strings of beads.

Houseware, hardware, wallpaper, and paint came.
Now it was time to give the store a name.
They stocked a variety of merchandise
So "variety store" was no surprise.

The Business of Business

You need someone to help you get started
But you're on your own when they have departed.
There are those who are willing to help you learn,
But first their confidence you will have to earn.

In business there is an old cliche—
It's "dog eat dog" and is still good today.
Each one is trying to get ahead,
But some will stay where they are instead.

There's just so much room on the ladder of success
And which one will make it is any one's guess.
There are some who get there by a recommend,
But when management changes their position will end.

Work hard and show that you are sincere
And willing to take on more each year.
It takes longer to reach your goal this way,
But once you are there you're more apt to stay.

Success is not the same for all,
For some think big and some think small.
Education too comes in various amounts,
But how it's applied is what really counts.

It is the ones at the top who have the say,
But it is the ones below who make it that way.

The Project

It wasn't meant to be big or small.
It was meant to be one size for all.
As it was being built it sort of grew.
No one seemed to know just what to do.

So the workers kept on building more
And it kept getting bigger than before.
It seemed to me it was getting out of hand,
But the workers didn't seem to understand.

Although there was no one to tell them to quit
Someone should know when they reach the end of it.
It's a nice project, as nice as you will find
And it certainly will be one of a kind.

The way things are going, it will turn out fine.
What is it, you ask? I don't know, it isn't mine.
Try as they may they couldn't find the owner.
Was this a joke or did someone pull a boner?

Snacking

Snacks are taken beween our meals
Regardless of how our stomach feels.
Snacks range from peanuts to pie and cake,
From chips and dips and things that we bake.

Candy, ice cream, lemonade and cheese
All go down with the greatest of ease.
Coffee, milk, hot chocolate and tea
Are snacks that taste good to you and me.

Then there is popcorn and fruit that we
Like to eat while watching T.V.
Chewing gum and all kinds of juice
Are other snacks that we may choose.

Peanut butter, pop, pretzels and beer,
even though dinner time is near.
Carmel corn, candy apples for all
We like to munch on every fall.

Most people try to stay on a diet
But snacks make them quit as soon as they try it.

Pickles in a Jar

Pickles, pickles in a jar
Oh, how very sweet they are.
Bread and butter pickles might
Whet a person's appetite.

Some think dill pickles are the best
And other folks can have the rest.
Sweet gherkins are the ones for me.
They're just what pickles ought to be.

Kosher pickles will be favored
By some and they will be savored.
Whenever you eat a pickle
Your taste buds it will tickle.

Any time that you want more
You can buy them at the store.
There are so many different kinds
It is hard to make up our minds.

Boughten pickles are a treat
But homemade pickles can't be beat.
Some prefer to make their own
For their family alone.

Pickles, pickles in a jar
You'll find them wherever you are.
So when company drops by
You'll have some for them to try.

Cruising

There are some who say cruisin's a sport
And some who say it's a last resort.
For those who seem to lack a "steady"
But who are willing and always ready

To meet someone that they admire
Whose friendship they would like to acquire,
Cruisin' is meant for the young at heart.
But there are others who do take part.

There are some who cruise just to join the crowd.
But most of them seem to be pretty loud.
And so the traffic goes to and fro
With those who have no place to go.

Competition

Competition began with man on this earth
I'll pass on to you for what it is worth.
Adam challenged the serpent and then Adam lost.
And when this happened just think what it cost.

God gave Adam a partner named Eve,
And when Adam lost, it caused them to leave
The Garden of Eden where they were to abide.
They could no longer live there for they lost their pride.

They didn't listen and didn't obey
And for that reason God sent them away.
Competition is something that is here to stay.
It's gone on through the ages and goes on today.

There were the cavemen who compete for their wives
And the gladiators who compete for their lives.
Then came the warriors to compete for the empire
To win as much land as each one could acquire.

The pirates sought fortune with murder and greed
To fill up their larders with more than they need.
And so it goes on all down through the years,
The winners are happy—the losers have tears.

Servicemen, lawyers, politicians, athlete—
Each one has been trained so they can compete.
Entertainers, policemen, and firemen too—
Each one of them knows just what they must do.

Hotels, real estate, schools and cafe—
They all try to turn competition their way.
T.V. stations, car dealers and even the store—
All vying for business for they all want more.

Competition is all pretty much the same—
Trying to win is the name of the game.

Sports

Hunting, fishing and golf are sports
That you will find in most resorts.
Bowling, pool and ping pong too
Gives us something else to do.

Outdoor sports are for the bold.
Indoor sports are for the old.
We throw the ball and the pins will fall—
Sometimes some and sometimes all.

The more that fall the better the score
So we try hard to knock down more.
We try again to knock down the pins
'Till someone loses and someone wins.

We hit the ball then walk up to it
And we wonder why we do it.
Each shot we make will be our best
And we will soon forget the rest.

The fewer shots the better the score
So we try hard to not make more.
Each one plays as he chooses
'Till someone wins and someone loses.

Professional Sports

Baseball, football, basketball bring the crowds into the stands
And they expect the players to meet all of their demands.
Anything less will bring the boos
And they will have to pay their dues.

Fans are loyal when the players play their best
But when they don't—well you know the rest.
They train and run and exercise until their body's sore,
Then they come back again next day and do it all some more.

The enormous salaries that they get tells their brain to do it,
And that's the only reason they are able to get through it.

Contests

Contests are to determine the best
The one who stands out from all the rest.
No matter how the judges may feel,
They must find one with the most appeal.

According to the rules that apply
And the categories they go by,
Competition for the beginner
Makes them sure they'll not be a winner.

Contests are great for those who send in.
Each has as much chance as the rest to win.
They make sure of their presentation
So they'll receive the acclamation.

That the one they enter will receive
If it has made the judges believe.
Contests are all pretty much the same.
Trying to win is the name of the game.

Point of View

The grass is always greener on the other side of the fence.
This is not necessarily true if we use our common sense.
If we go on the other side and look at ours today,
We will see to our surprise ours will look the very same way.

If you stare at something long enough, it will appear to move.
But when you look away and then look back it still is in the
groove.
Look at fish under water and they will seem to be long.
But when you take them out and look, it will prove that you
were wrong.

In the desert, looking from afar, an oasis will appear.
But as you travel on your way, it's a mirage when you get
near.
When you look toward a mountain it will look very near.
But when you finally reach it, you'll be a long time getting
here.

Look at the telephone poles as you are driving by one day.
They are the ones that are moving—you're just sitting along
the way.
Looking down the railroad tracks, they seem to change
position.
They come together at the other end, which is a strange
condition.

When the hot sun shines on water, it looks like rising whisps
of smoke.
Actually it is like a mirage and one of nature's jokes.
It's hard to believe blizzards come from the tiny snowflakes
that fall.
But with the help of a little wind they can do it all.

Looking into a mirror, things are on the opposite side then,
But when we turn and look the other way things are right
     again.
Stand a pencil in a glass of water and the refraction you will
     get.
The pencil will be in two parts and the parts will be offset.

The Family Album

The family album what does it contain?
Pictures of course which will always remain.
It also contains records of all sorts
Such as achievements in all kinds of sports.

Pages that have long since turned yellow with age,
Our parents wedding picture on the front page,
Then parents and children in their finest clothes
Arranged where the photographer asked them to pose.

Grandparents, aunts, uncles, family members all,
Nieces, nephews, cousins that we can recall,
Pictures of families from way back when
That we like to look at again and again.

Then comes the grandchildren and their families.
The children all looking like they have just said "cheeze"
They try to get them all to look their best
But some will look crazy like you might have guessed.

Pictures of birthdays, anniversaries too,
Reunions and weddings of people we knew.
Pictures of friends and neighbors that we have met,
We write down all their names so we won't forget.

Trips and vacations, all the pictures we took
Neatly arranged in one section of the book.
The album contains quite a few candid shots
Catching the people alone with their thoughts.

So much of our lifetime we didn't record
Because it was something we couldn't afford,
Or we forgot to bring our cameras along,
Or the film and flash bulbs we bought were wrong.

We never can get them all in one album
So we will to use more than one volume.
There's merit certificates we earned in school,
Marriage license as a general rule,

Birth certificates and all sorts of papers,
Some notes and memos from some of our capers.
You might think these belong in a scrap book
But these are in among some pictures we took.

They go together to record each event,
The things we did and the places we went.
Thus what we do have brings us much pleasure.
The family album is truly a treasure.

Books

Professional's shelves are full of books.
They're not there just for their looks.
It took them many years of learning
To get the money that they're earning.

One day they'll save somebody's life.
Next day they'll help somebody's wife.
Problems seem to be abounding
And some seem to be astounding.

Just one match can start some fires.
Too many drinks that one desires
Can cause trouble anywhere,
So people must be made aware.

It's from books that children learn.
Some day it will be their turn
To teach the children all these things—
Reading, writing and how to sing.

And worldly things that they must know
So they will know which way to go.
Books contain a wealth of knowledge
For these who want to go to college.

Some books are meant just for reading.
But don't let that be misleading.
Poems and stories of all kind—
These are meant to ease the mind.

Dictionaries, encyclopedias, and cook books
For the students and the cooks.
They need these books for reference too
Everyday their whole life through.

The Bible too must have its place
on the shelf or the bookcase.
It is needed for the way
That it comforts us each day.

Books of first or second editions
Are not valued for their conditions.
You can see books are a treasure
To have for learning or just pleasure.

Elections — The American Way

It is such a beautiful day,
We all go to the park and play.
After we go to church to pray,
That is the real American way.

We honor our flag in a special way,
And honor God whenever we pray.
This we do almost every day.
That is the real American way.

We listen to what the candidates say
And the message that each tries to convey.
We do this before election day.
That is the real American way.

Campaign managers think smearing's the way
To get some people's votes to sway.
How dumb do they think we are, anyway?
That is *not* the American way.

With the two party system of today
The issues we must carefully weigh
And their character, too, without delay.
That is called the American way.

Then when it comes to election day,
We must make a choice and not stay away.
We mark our ballot and have our say.
That is the *real* American way.

Michigan

Michigander or Michiganese
Why must we be called one of these?
Why not just plain Michigans?
This tells all that we are fans.

Of all the activities and all the beauty
And we must hold that it's our duty
To spread the word to all each day
That this is where we wish to stay.

The opportunities here are great
For those who have the time to wait.
There are industries from border to border.
You can find employment that's made to order.

But employment is only part of our scheme.
To fulfill the rest of our dream,
To see the whole State in all its glory,
For this is the whole point of this story.

California

There was a truly fine life in California.
I have a truly dear wife in California.
I have many wonderful friends in California.
But that's where my true love ends for California.

People

The Family

A religious institution
Which has found the right solution
To the problems of each day
Love and devotion is the way.

As the family grows it changes.
Our style of life rearranges.
Our children must obey the rules
When we send them off to school.

The knowledge that they'll attain
And the friendships they will gain
Are things they'll need their whole life through
For almost everything they do.

Now they have families of their own,
And their parents are left alone
Except the grandchildren that are there
Who have been left in their loving care.

The Twelve Lives of Motherhood

Matriarch
Organizer
Teacher
Homemaker
Energizer
Rewarder

Discipliner
Pacifier
Adhesive (holds family together)
Financial genius
Doctor
Jack-of-all trades (and master of some)

She's the one you know as mother
Who is truly like no other.

Childbirth

The miracle of childbirth to a husband and wife
Is one of God's plans, the continuance of life.
He will call someone home and while we still mourn
Somewhere to someone a baby is born.

They will change your style of life but think of the joy.
No matter if it's a girl or if it's a boy.
All through their lives there'll be worry and heartache,
For we never know which road each will take.

Never give up on a child of your own,
No matter how bad they seem when alone.
It's possible if they should go the wrong way
They might turn about and return home to stay.

The love that you give them will come back tenfold
Later on in life when you're growing old.

A Mother's Love and Duty

A Mother's love and duty could be one and the same.
The situations are alike with just a different name.
Mothers are not here on earth just for their beauty.
God made a place for them so they could do their duty.

To raise their family and make them wise and strong,
To teach them what they need for them to get along,
To teach them the fundamentals of what life should be,
To teach each one according to their ability.

So they will know what to do when they are on their own,
To let them know that they will never be alone.
They calm our fears, wipe our tears and make them go away.
They hold us tight in the night and calm us with things they
    say.

Mothers express their love in many thoughtful ways,
And tears are shed for each of us whenever she prays.
Mothers are like flowers in a garden of weeds.
They always seem to know just what the family needs.

Mothers are like music that goes floating through the air.
When you need someone to talk to they are always there.
Mothers are like poems with their beauty and their grace.
When it comes to the family, no one can take their place.

Grandmother

Another lady to behold,
Full of charm and grace I am told,
I didn't know her personally
But those who did, found her to be

Filled with strength and fidelity
And wisdom to capacity.
Guardian of her small domain
She had the privilege to reign.

She was gentle, kind and just
In her new position of trust.
Her decisions were always fair
For those who were under her care.

Unusual as this may seem,
It was really not a dream,
Nor was it a fantasy
But it really happened to be.

The Grandma I had never known
Who was now left all alone
To care for those as best she could
But Grandpa always knew she would.

Grandpa

It seemed like only yesterday
That I held you on my knee.
You were just a little tad
And lively as you could be.

Then while you were growing up
We weren't together very much
And as the years kept going by
Somehow it seems that we lost touch.

Although we seem so far apart
I remember a little lad
Freckled face and tousled hair
And recall the good times we had.

It was so many years ago
They tell me now that you are grown
And have been married quite some time
And have children of your own.

Grandpa needs this information
That began so long ago
To put in the family album
Things the family ought to know.

Runaways

A person belongs to those who brought
Them into this world and they cannot deny it.
But the world is full of runaway children
Who just felt they had to try it.

Placing the blame is not the answer once
They are out there on their own.
If they call a hot-line and talk to someone,
They'll let them know they're not alone.

There is nothing you can do but pray as you
Wait with a heavy heart.
But you can't help wondering what it was
That caused them to depart.

Statistics show that once they go they're
Not likely to return.
This doesn't help the feeling you have
That causes you concern.

Don't ever give up the feeling you have
And continue with your prayer.
It's possible that one day they might
Return to your loving care.

Teenage Years

Teenagers are children who have yet to mature.
They're still in between and do not feel secure.
From adolescence to grown-up seems like so long.
To get through this stage they have to be strong.

So much going on in these in between years.
There is so much sorrow and so many tears.
They seem to be thoughtless but really they're not.
With so much on their minds they simply forgot.

There are proms and parties and dances galore
And dates with friends—need I say more?
Their learning begins as soon as they're born,
And without education they're looked on with scorn.

They should learn much from their mother and dad.
There's a wealth of information from them to be had.
And as they mature they should stay in school,
For school may be used as a learning tool.

Now it is time to go look for work.
It is a responsibility they must not shirk.
But some will choose a different life
And want to be somebody's wife

Or husband as the case may be,
For each one has a choice you see.
Teenagers would all like to turn out well,
And most of them do as near as I can tell.

Being a teenager is so hard to do.
I would not want to be one and neither would you.

Preparation

She must get up a little early
Just in case her hair's too curly.
First she gets into the shower
For she only has an hour.

Then she fixes up her hair
And lays out what she will wear.
Now she must put on her face.
This cannot be done in haste.

Basic makeup she'll apply,
Then some color to each eye.
Now she puts on what she'll wear,
Careful not to muss her hair.

One quick look before she goes
To make sure that nothing shows.
Some things were done way ahead
Just before she went to bed.

She looks around just to make sure
That everything will be secure.
Now that there is nothing more,
She'll make sure to lock the door.

Then to start and warm the car
She doesn't have to drive too far.
She doesn't want to get there late,
But she's not due to start till eight.

The Lady of the House

"Are you the lady of the house?" you hear them say so much.
And if she's not, then you might find you could be "in Dutch."
But if she has a sense of humor you could be O.K.
For she might say to "come on in" instead of "go away."

The lady of the house is the matriarch who runs the family's
    affair,
And of this the family members have all become aware.
She has joined up with the neighbors to form a driving pool
To take turns with the others getting the kids to school.

She goes to the grocery store to buy the family food.
She does this once or twice a week to feed her hungry brood.
She makes them all their breakfast to start them on their way,
Then works on the other meals that she will serve that day.

While she cleans the house, she does the laundry too.
Seems like there will always be something more to do.
She turns on the TV to watch the story's ending.
This is when she finds the time to do the family mending.

She attends her clubs, for her social life,
To relieve the stress of her daily strife.
She doesn't just work from sun to sun,
The lady of the house is never done.

The Waiting Game

Now that she was in her teens
She wore mostly sweaters and jeans.
She seemed more popular than most
But she was never one to boast.

Like her age, her beauty grew
And her popularity too.
She wore dresses to suit her age
As her life turned another page.

There were lots of dates and dinners
And some dances with some winners.
She liked the ones that she would date,
But wouldn't want them for a mate.

She was anxious to be wed
But she'd wait awhile instead.
The years passed by faster now.
Still she might make it yet somehow.

There was one she liked a lot,
That she had almost forgot.
She could call him on the phone.
Maybe he would be alone.

He did appreciate her call.
It would be no trouble at all
To get together once again,
If he would know just where and when.

After meeting a time or two
It seemed to be the thing to do.
And since they each needed a friend,
No reason now for it to end.

Thus a courtship started to grow.
Where it might end no one could know.
It just happened, they knew not how,
They decided to marry now.

The long wait for each has ended.
Now the two lives have been blended.
It is better late than never
And we hope it lasts forever.

The Weary Traveler

O weary traveler come sit a spell.
We know you must have some tales to tell
Of places you've been, and things you've done
And you can recall them one by one.

O weary traveler come and find rest.
Come sup with us and we will be blest.
We shall bid you good-night until the morn.
Our wish for you is to not feel forlorn.

O weary traveler fresh as this new day
Tend to your needs then we bid you to stay.
Tell us how you got started to roam.
What are your feelings so far from home.

Tell us the tales that you can recall.
To travelers our little world must seem small.
Tell us of places we've never heard.
We're eager to know and will not miss a word.

O weary traveler you will be missed.
We'd like you to stay—in fact we insist.
Well when you put it that way I might
Stay another day and one more night.

When you good folks awaken at dawn
Do not search for me for I shall be gone.
It is time for me to be on my way.
I shall remember you folks each day.

The Undoing of Doctor Little

The good doctor's ride to the ship that day
Was a little too fast along the way.
But he was anxious to board the ship
That would take him on another trip.

Many times he made it before
And each time he seemed to enjoy it more.
But this time the doctor found that he
Had a poorly equipped infirmary.

It's hard enough to attend the sick.
With this equipment it's quite a trick.
But a ship's doctor can't pick and choose.
He will work with what he has to use.

The weather was calm and the ship steady.
He had the feeling that he was ready.
This trip he was sure would be O.K.
Once they were able to get under way.

The ship was seaworthy despite its age
If the sea didn't go into a rage.
The experienced seamen who should know
Felt the ship was ready to go.

One day the ship began to pitch and roll.
Before long it started to take its toll
And the infirmary started to fill
With the seamen who had become ill.

Experienced seamen becoming sea-sick,
They came in so fast he just took his pick.
All he could do was give them a pill
And hope no one came that was really ill.

This continued for several days more.
They were too far away from the shore,
So he had to grit his teeth and bear it.
There was no one with whom he could share it.

When it was over he needed some rest.
Everyone knew he had done his best,
But when he laid down he got sea-sick too.
Now no one seemed to know what to do.

The good doctor Little had it real bad,
And that is the thing that makes it so sad.
Whenever this happened to him, he knew
That his ship doctoring days were through.

He finished the cruise and did what he could
To ease the suffering for those who would
Come in the infirmary for their pain.
He'd treat them and send them back again.

Doctor Little always knew that he
Would never again go out to sea.
If he ever got sea-sick on a ship,
It would have to be his very last trip.

Marriage

Wedding bells don't tell the story,
Nor the love in all it's glory.

You love each other, that is true,
And you both love others too.

But it's the things you say and do
That make it last your whole life through.

Double Trouble

Out of the gutter into the mire,
Out of the frying pan into the fire.

Now you have one more chance to make it.
Aren't you glad you are able to take it?

Cops

To call all lawmen cops we should object.
They should be treated with more respect.

They put their life on the line for others.
They all do their jobs like they were our brothers.

There is only one lawman who should be called cop,
That's the **C**hief **O**f **P**olice, he's the one at the top.

The Forgiving Father

Wouldst thou attend the ball with me, he asked with a bow
I wouldst go with thee, if father would allow.
I shall ask him forthwith if thee might go with me.
If thee return ere midnight I shall trust her with thee.

I thank thee very much and we will be home ere twelve.
I shall mind the time and shall see to it myself.
I rented a one horse shay which had only one seat.
We drove to a wayside inn for something to eat.

Whither goest thou, queried the keeper of the inn.
We shall attend the ball if we're able to get in.
Then a leisurely drive took us on to the ball.
The place looked awfully full like it wouldn't hold us all.

The room was overcrowded and hard to get around.
Space large enough to dance on was so hard to be found.
Then more people came to dance later on that night
So push came to shove and some of them began to fight.

We worked our way through the crowd and started home at
    last
But by the time we got home it was a quarter past.
Father was waiting and said I'll trust thee no more.
Thee shall take thy leave and make sure thee close the door.

We tried to explain but he had nothing more to say.
There was nothing left for me but to be on my way.
Daughter was able to explain the situation.
We looked forward to meet with great anticipation.

Father relented and forgave us for being late
So I was able once again to ask her for a date.
It was an enjoyable friendship right from the start.
We miss each other very much when we are apart.

Wouldst thou marry me if I seek father's permission?
I wouldst marry thee but there is one condition.
The wedding must be small with just family attending
And our love so true that it will be never ending.

So with father's permission the nuptial took place.
The bride was bedecked with veil and dress of silk and lace.
Then father gave the bride away and the vows were read.
When the reverend said kiss the bride, we knew we were wed.

Everybody's Somebody

Everybody's somebody
From the smallest to the great.
Even those in prison
Who are filled with so much hate.

Everybody's somebody.
Those held in detention
Have committed crimes
Just to get someone's attention.

Everybody's somebody.
And God can help them all
If they will only let Him
From the greatest to the small.

Everybody's somebody
No matter what their race.
No one should be overlooked
Because of our fast pace.

Everybody's somebody
Regardless of lifestyle.
The less that people have,
The more apt they are to smile.

Everybody's somebody
No matter who they be.
Everybody's somebody—
Even you and me.

Friendship

There was a girl named Kelly
Who knew a girl named Nelly
Between the two
A friendship grew
Like peanut butter and jelly.

There was a boy named Larry
Who knew a girl named Carry.
Between the two
A friendship grew
So they decided to marry.

There was a boy named Will
Who knew a girl named Jill,
And a boy named Wayne
Who knew a girl named Jayne.
Will liked Jayne,
Jill liked Wayne,
So they made an exchange.

Friends

Most friends are like the seasons.
They will come and go away.
But the friends that mean so much to us
Are the ones who come to stay.

We miss the ones who move away
And try to keep in touch.
But through the years the way we live
It seems to be too much.

We remember all the happy times
We had when they were near,
And we think how nice that it would be
If only they were here.

To renew the friendship we once knew
A letter we will send,
So we may once again be friends
And may our friendship never end.

Friends are priceless and can't be bought
With either silver or gold,
And friends are wonderful to have
When we are growing old.

I'll Leave It Up To You

It's not exactly moonlight
But it'll have to do.
It's not exactly June light,
But it's up to you

To do a little dancing
And pitch a little woo,
Maybe some romancing
Meant for just us two.

I'm not sure why you are
So lovely that is true.
I have been near and far,
But I have seen no one who

Would be someone that I
Could compare you to.
So I guess I won't try
And just leave it up to you.

The Natural Instinct of Man

I have to agree with Shakespeare when he said something
 like:
"All the world's a stage and players everyone that's in it."
And P. T. Barnum who said, "There's one born every minute."
Referring to those who like to play the games of chance
Who are certain they have them figured out in advance.

Gambling has a tendency to really fascinate some.
Others get the fever that they can never overcome.
We are all players acting out each day of our lives.
But one might not make it and the other one survives.

Which one of us will make it there is no way of knowing.
The ones that make it are not sure where they are going.
And so after all when everything is said and done
We just can't help wondering if we could be the one.

We might wonder why we differ from all the others.
Even from our parents, our sisters, and our brothers.
But we all play our part in our lives as best we can.
That is because it's the natural instinct of man.

Shutterbugs

There are lots of things to write about
And there are a lot of things to see.
Camera buffs are interesting people.
They take pictures for posterity.

They can't just point the camera and shoot.
Locating the subject must be done.
Not all subjects are in the center
Whether it be a group or just one.

Taking pictures is a special art.
They must see the picture in their mind,
How it will look when it's developed
From the best angle they can find.

Backgrounds must blend in with the subject,
And there must be no reflection glare.
Pictures of people are hard to get
To show expression without the stare.

Pictures of events where there are crowds
Have to be taken with candid shots.
The object is to show the highlights
And try to capture the people's thoughts.

Scenery pictures must always be
Interesting to others as well.
So they must carefully weigh the scene
For the story that it will tell.

They should be self explanatory.
Pictures are meant to be a pleasure
For those to see when they're not around
Because pictures are truly a treasure.

Your Doctor

Doctors are just like you and me
Except they have a different degree.
They have to deal with philosophy
As well as with reality.

Two kinds of pain with which they must deal—
Psychosomatic and that which is real.
They must distinguish between the two
And sometimes that is very hard to do.

There are times doctors have to rely
On their experience what to try.
Their instincts tell them which way to go
In cases where they do not know.

The way that you describe your ailment
Helps them find a way of curtailment.
It's their only way to diagnose
For a treatment they can propose.

That's why they run so many tests
To confirm what they may have guessed.
It seems like the doctors take so long
To let you know what might be wrong.

If they find that it's an infection,
Then they will give you an injection.
If it's something else and they're not sure,
They'll not give up till they find a cure.

Doctors are human after all
And ready to serve you when you call.
The Hippocratic Oath will ensure
The many problems they endure

Will keep them searching for a new way
To treat a problem a patient may
Come in to see if they can find
A cure for a problem of their kind.

Doctors seem to have that special touch,
But they can only do so much.
They will always do their very best,
Then it's up to you to do the rest.

Your Dentist

When you go to the dentist and sit in his chair
You're already shaking before you get there.
Just remember it only hurts for a while,
And when he is done you'll be able to smile.

You think to yourself, that wasn't so bad,
And now you're all over the feeling you had.
An appointment for your next checkup you make
To let your teeth go would be a mistake.

He is there to help when your teeth give you pain,
But also to keep them from hurting again.
So see your dentist at least once a year,
Now that you know there is nothing to fear.

Your Barber

Everyone thinks their barber's the best.
They cut their hair better than the rest.
Some people go by the time it takes,
Others go by the difference it makes.

Some barbers don't seem to really care
About the people who come in there.
Others are willing to chat awhile
And always give a cheerful smile.

They take care of the little ones too,
Just like their own parents would do.
Getting a haircut can be pleasant
Depending on the barber present.

It isn't the amount of time it took,
It's when they are through how it will look.
For a haircut with a special price
Barber students will cut it real nice.

So you see there are many choices,
And you will hear from many voices,
Each one saying their barber's the best.
They'll cut your hair better than the rest.

The Postal Service

The postman doesn't ring at all anymore
When they deliver the mail from door to door.
There are ways to tell when they're making their rounds,
The barking of dogs and the mailbox sounds.

They carry the mailbag on their shoulder
Or use a cart when they get older.
They pick up the letters that need to be mailed,
A part of their job that they never have failed.

Of course this just applies to the ones in town.
The rural carriers are just as renown.
Although they are able to work from a car,
Their routes are laid out so they reach pretty far.

Both have a problem fitting the mail in the box,
But they both seem to get very few squawks,
For you see they each sort the mail for their route.
They know what goes where as they sort it all out.

Handling the mail is a responsible task
And not always pleasant if one should ask.
The weather plays tricks and is not always nice.
Sometimes there's rain and then again snow and ice.

Mail that goes in the P. O. Boxes inside
Is handled by postal clerks who do it with pride.
They work inside but there are only a few
So they never run out of something to do.

Working the window sometimes makes them nervous
But that is just one part of their service.
They prepare the mail for the outgoing sack
So it goes where it should and will not come back.

Seems like they all do a lot of extra giving,
But after all that's how they make their living.

Senior Bowlers

Seniors are just children at heart
Longing for a second start.
We all gather in a bunch.
We bowl and then we go to lunch.

Bowling fills a need in our lives—
A need for us to socialize.
We talk about things that we learn
While we are waiting for our turn.

Seniors are not bowling pros.
We make mistakes and it just shows
We are able to take our lumps
When we go into our slumps.

When good friends get together
We don't talk about the weather
For we're here for just one reason
At the end of bowling season.

Reflecting on what each has done
It makes no difference which team won.
Looking back on each team's past
One team has to finish last.

Special
Occasions

Birthdays

We invite all our friends and all of our neighbors.
We wear crazy hats and have lots of favors.
We play silly games, drink punch and eat cake.
I think I have had about all I can take.

We wish them all well and bid them adieu.
We wipe our brow and say we're glad it's through.
When we are young it seems like fun, I guess,
But when we get older it seems like a mess.

Birthdays for Seniors

Birthdays are not as important now as they were when we
    were small,
But it's better to have them anyway than not have them at all.
Birthdays are the milestones of our life that show what we
    have done—
Our accomplishments and failures—and as we count them one
    by one.

We find that as each year goes by, there are lessons that we
    learn.
And some will be a surprise to us and give us much concern.
We seem to forget from year to year, for they go by so fast,
The things that happened the years before that have already
    passed.

But all in all as we get older and look back from year to year,
The many blessings we received that helped get us up to here,
We remember on this birthday and give thanks we've come
    this far.
Then we realize to our surprise just how far along we are.

Banquets

Banquets are social celebrations
Or for business delegations.
They meet to hold the past in review
And go over the things that are new.

Awards are given out for merit,
Certificates for those who share it.
It's a time for fun and laughter
And memories that follow after.

The food has been prepared in advance
So nothing would be left to chance.
Whenever there's a large meeting,
There's always trouble with the seating.

Once everyone has found a chair,
The speaker will offer up a prayer.
Now the waiters can serve the food
For everyone is in the mood.

Spring Proms

Spring proms will be taking place
All across our nation.
It just happens once a year,
This special occasion.

This creates a problem.
They'd better not be late
If they plan on taking
A very special date.

Some will wear tuxedos.
Some have to draw the line.
So they will wear their suits
And they will look just fine.

Some girls will buy their gowns.
Some make the ones they'll wear.
They will all look good enough
To take them anywhere.

All proms have their chaperones
To monitor the proms,
So folks don't have to worry—
especially their moms.

They will dance the night away
And then go out to eat.
As tired as they all are,
To sit down will be a treat.

Now it's time to take them home.
It's hard for them to start.
They may never meet again
Once they have gone apart.

There'll be joy for most of them
And sadness for the rest.
Some thought it was the saddest
But most thought it was the best.

The Concert

Whoa there, Missy, What's your rush?
Gotta catch the early bus.
Gonna hear the great one sing
And watch the others do their thing.

I hear the line's already forming.
Very soon they'll be performing.
They'll be here from every state.
No one wants to miss this date.

It's a once in a lifetime thing to see,
So it's where everyone wants to be.
There'll be laughter and much fun
For he is truly number one.

Easter Time

It's almost time for Easter
And the bunny's on its nest.
This is where the eggs come from
Just like you might have guessed.

Easter time is a happy time
And a sad time, too.
It's happy for the children
And sad for me and you.

The way Jesus had to die
To save us from our sin,
But when He arose again,
It made us warm within.

So we dress up in our finest
And go to church to pray
To give thanks to Him who died for us
On the cross that day.

Easter

Easter is a time to mourn
The death of Jesus who was born
To suffer on the cross that day
To rid us of our sin that way.

It was His own life that He gave,
Then they placed Him in a cave.
In three days He arose alone.
The angels rolled away the stone.

When He appeared they knew Him not.
It was not that they forgot.
They assumed that He was dead,
But there He stood with them instead.

In the spirit He ascended
But His story hasn't ended,
For by faith we still believe
If we ask, we shall receive.

Saint Patrick's Day

The reason we celebrate Saint Patrick's Day,
He is the one who showed the Irish the way
To Christianity and close contact with Rome.
Born in western Britain, he made Ireland his home.

Son of a Christian deacon, he was made a slave.
Irish raiders made him a shepherd with a stave.
About six years later he escaped into Gaul,
Became a monk, then in a dream he got the call

To convert the Irish to the Christian ways.
Appointed bishop, he served the rest of his days.
Legend says in Ireland he drove out the snakes
That the power of sainthood was all that it takes.

The shamrock's three leaves illustrate the trinity—
The Father, Son and Holy Ghost of divinity.
The patron saint and apostle of Ireland,
His feast day, March 17, all Irish understand.

School Daze

Students are never ready
No matter when school begins.
It isn't the schooling they mind,
It's the confinement within.

After a summer of leisure
Doing things they want to do
Once their classes have started
Their life of leisure is through.

Most students try to adjust
Still there seems to be a few
That simply can't or won't try
To adjust to something new.

They move into a higher grade
That's harder than the one before.
They'll have to give up some free time
To be able to study more.

There are some students who will be
Preparing to go to college.
The main thing they will have to learn
Is how to obtain their knowledge.

So for the first few days of school
It is hard to get started.
They renew the friendships they had
Last year when they departed.

College Days

There are those who are able to go to college
With the opportunity to gain more knowledge
And improve their social life while they are there.
Of their appearance too they'll be made more aware.

It's not like high school where they were told what to do.
Teachers discuss what they're to learn then it's up to you.
It's the ones with ambition that will get ahead,
But there are those who would rather socialize instead.

It's a shame more students aren't able to find a way.
Some do go to school at night and work through the day.
There are those with scholarships who go just for the sports.
When they look about the campus they will see all sorts.

Basic knowledge is not the only thing they learn.
Extra activities have credits they can earn.
There's cheerleader, gym, choral group, band, track and such,
But they must be careful that they don't do too much.

They'll be making friends with people they never knew
Until they came to college and a friendship grew.
They must choose very carefully who their friends will be.
For in college, lifetime friendships can be made, you see.

Valentines

There are 14 ways to say that I love you.
There are 14 ways to say you love me too.
There are 14 ways to say just how we feel.
There are 14 ways to show our love is real.

We'll have 14 days to show it's true
And 14 ways to say we're through.
There are 14 different ways to show
We're just a bit too young to know.

At 14 years our lives have just begun.
It's time for us to go and have some fun.
So tell the world so everyone will know,
That both of us our separate ways must go.

To those who like to read between the lines,
You know that we were only "Valentines."

Valentines

Have you ever wished we were kids again?
Valentines seemed so important then.
I remember the names that we drew
So we would know who ours would go to.

Then there were always the special girls.
One had dimples—the other had curls.
There were the boys that girls hardly knew
They would like to send valentines to.

The teacher would always get the best.
Sometimes we would make all the rest.
Sometimes we'd buy the penny kind
And pick out the best ones we could find.

We would always make one for our mother,
One more special than any other.
It all began with Saint Valentine's Day.
Since then we express our love this way.

Vacation

First the planning must be done
So we all will have some fun.
Then our maps we study over
So we know what roads to cover.

As our clothes we sort to pack,
We find what we must put back.
Games and racquets, golf clubs too,
So we all have things to do.

Next the car we have to check
So we don't get in a wreck.
Gas and oil we must fill,
Then we need to pay the bill.

Ask our neighbor yet today
To watch our home while we're away.
Get up early in the morning,
Dress up to go without a warning.

Time to leave was set before
So when it's time, we'll close the door.
The sun is rising as we leave.
It's beauty makes us all believe

That we are really on our way
And we will have a real nice day.
All along the countryside
Are homes where country folks reside.

Everywhere we look it's green
Like nothing we have ever seen.
Here comes a town where we will stop,
Gas up the car and get some pop.

Go to the restroom one by one
'Til all have gone and we're all done.
'Tis almost noon and time to eat.
Let's all go in and have a seat.

Order only what you wish
So when it comes out on a dish
You'll eat it all and not be wasteful.
It's what you like because it's tasteful.

So now we'll journey on our way
Until we finally end the day,
Have dinner in a small cafe
Then look for a place to stay.

To bed we'll go to get some rest
So in the morn we'll look our best
To travel yet another day
And reach the place we want to stay.

We visit with relatives and friends,
We air our views and make amends,
We play our games and do our thing
And hope that happiness we'll bring.

To those who join us in the game
And to the rest of those who came
Now our allotted time has ended
And we hope no one's offended.

So to all goodbye we say
For we must be on our way.
As we journey homeward bound
It's the same thing we have found.

As the trip we made this way,
As we drive along each day,
We have lost our wish to roam.
We just want to reach our home.

Time to unload the car you know.
Now where did everybody go?
To the bathroom one by one
until the work has all been done.

Vacation by Air

We must get up early to make the long drive
So we won't be late when we do arrive.
We say our goodbyes when it's time to go.
Now our tickets and seat number we must show.

People are friendly whenever they fly
So it doesn't matter who we sit by.
It's like the man on the flying trapeze
As we fly thru the air with the greatest of ease.

They give us a snack and something to drink.
This gives us a chance to sit back and think.
We notice the clouds as we go flying past.
It seems like we're traveling awfully fast.

There'll be someone to meet us when we arrive,
Then through all the traffic we have to drive.
We finally arrive at our destination
Which we've looked to with anticipation.

We visit our relation and all of our friends
Then all too soon our vacation time ends.
Once again we must get our reservation and seat
Then like before once again we repeat.

Drive to the airport and get on the plane
So we can fly back home once again.
We'll be met at the airport when we arrive,
Then once again we must make the long drive.

Now we arrive at home once again.
Wouldn't you know it, it's starting to rain.
Now that we're home we really don't care,
For we don't intend to go anywhere.

Camping

We meant to dry the tent from our last trip
And mend the place where it had a big rip.
We rinsed it off but it still smells musty
And the rest of our gear is all dusty.

We unrolled and shook all our sleeping bags
And dusted the rest off with some old rags.
We checked everything and it was all there
Plus what we will eat and what we will wear.

We check it again each thing as we pack,
Even the things that are on the top rack.
We set up our tent and get settled in.
Wouldn't you know it? You just cannot win.

There is one more thing that we all forgot—
The mosquito repellent wasn't brought.
Maybe they will not be as bad this year.
There is one now buzzing around my ear.

Now it is time to prepare our dinner.
We think this outing will be a winner.
We light our lantern so we can retire,
Or just sit around beside the campfire.

We wonder after we sit for an hour
Where are the restrooms and where is the shower?
Where are the blankets? The nights get quite cool.
They are in the backyard beside the pool.

Oh well, after all, on our camping trips,
We're entitled to a couple of slips.
Soon we will get what we're all looking for,
Some excitement for it's starting to pour.

We run for our tent so we will be cozy,
Then a family of skunks start to get nosy.
If we don't try to scare them away,
Maybe they'll decide they don't want to stay.

They have found out now the food is all gone.
They've decided now and are moving on.
There are chipmunks, squirrels, and birds galore
And some of them come right up to our door.

The next few days we have lots of fun.
Most of the time we are on a dead run.
It is time now to break camp and return.
There is one thing though that gives us concern.

We have forgotten to gas up the car.
With what we have we won't get very far.
There must be a station on the campground.
There is and it's the only one around.

We head for home with no more delays
And unpack our camper just like always.
Despite our mistakes we enjoyed it all,
So we'll no doubt do it again next fall.

Short Vacation

God speed you on your way
Though you're not going to stay
You can't keep from showing
The excitement of going.

I wish you good weather
While you are together.
So much to do and to say
You'll be busy every day.

Seeing friends and having fun—
That will keep you on the run.
Going here and going there
Leaves you no time to spare.

Vacation time goes so fast
And you wish that it would last.
So much you'd like to achieve,
But it's time for you to leave.

Give them all your fond goodbyes
And dry the tears from your eyes.
Give a smile that's from the heart
And a wave as you depart.

Wanderlust

I don't care where I am going just as long as I get there.
There are people going here and there and going everywhere.
We all have the wanderlust and like to travel around.
Some of them like to fly—others like to stay on the ground.

There are those who go for pleasure and they like to go on
　　ships.
Others prefer to take the train when they go on their trips.
There's another way to travel, you can always take the bus.
Of course there's the reliable old car for the rest of us.

Some folks have never traveled so they don't know what
　　they're missing.
They sit at home and watch T.V. and then end up just wishing.
Now there's no excuse to stay at home and wish your life
　　away.
So pick up your phone and call around to make your plans
　　today.

Jack-O-Lantern

Jack-O-Lantern is a pumpkin with a face
For Hallowe'en, nothing can take its place.
Some have a smile—some have a frown,
But that is a smile when turned upside down.

It is the symbol of Hallowe'en,
And at most of the homes one can be seen.
Jack-O-Lanterns always vary in size.
Sometimes the best one is awarded a prize.

Cleaning out the pumpkin is quite a mess,
But it's part of the fun for most I guess.
Making the cutouts is really the most fun
And it can be done by most anyone.

With the candle inside it looks real neat
To those who come to trick or treat.
This ritual continues every fall
And is enjoyed by one and all.

As the Months Go By

January	February	March
Carnation	Violet	Jonquil
Garnet	Amethyst	Bloodstone
Capricornus	Aquarius	Pisces
(The Goat)	(The Water Bearer)	(The Fishes)

April	May	June
Sweet Pea	Lily of the Valley	Rose
Diamond	Emerald	Pearl
Aries	Taurus	Gemini
(The Ram)	(The Bull)	(The Twins)

July	August	September
Larkspur	Gladiolus	Aster
Ruby	Sardonyx	Sapphire
Cancer	Leo	Virgo
(The Crab)	(The Lion)	(The Virgin)

October	November	December
Calendula	Chrysanthemum	Narcissus
Opal	Topaz	Turquoise
Libra	Scorpio	Sagittarius
(The Scales)	(The Scorpion)	(The Archer)

January ushers in the year with promises to break
With hopes high for a better year by changes we can make.

February finds us looking forward with anticipation
For the end of the winter snow that gives us consternation.

March with its wind and blustery weather is still better than
　　snow.
Though it still holds the winter chill, we bundle up and let it
　　blow.

April gives us the feeling of spring, though it may rain a lot
It helps us later when we are ready to plant the seeds we
　　bought.

May brings us the flowers from the seeds and plants we set out
So now we know spring is here at last without any doubt.

June The traditional month of weddings with bridal veils and
　　flowers
And preparations to be made including all the showers.

July is a summer month so it is naturally hot,
And celebrating our independence must not be forgot.

August is vacation time for those who have children in school,
Then shop for the clothes and things they need as a general
　　rule.

September we celebrate Labor Day and the beginning of fall
And the beginning of school again for students, teachers and
　　all.

October gives us a new look as nature does its duty
Changing the colors all around to show us its fall beauty.

November we offer a prayer to thank God for the harvest we
   reap.
We will can most of it and prepare the rest so that it will keep.

December brings the winter chill and the heavy clothing we
   wear.
We celebrate the birth of Jesus and thank God in prayer.

The Holiday Season

Labor Day is the last outdoor fling of the year
Except for those who go hunting for the deer.
Thanksgiving with all its fall colors and such
Is the day that we're always eating too much.

We give our thanks and each offers a prayer
For all the ones who are not able to be there.
The holiday season is a festive affair.
You can see it glowing almost everywhere.

Colored lights and garlands dressing up the street,
People saying hello to all of those they meet.
They seem to be smiling and friendlier too
And are shaking more hands than they normally do.

There are parades and bands both large and small
To celebrate the greatest holiday of all.
Twinkling lights and fancy wreaths will dress up each home
To welcome all the others that they know will come.

Again we will gather at the table to eat
And it will be another wonderful treat.
Then there will be football to watch for those who care,
Card games or just visiting for the others who are there.

Some will be showing off the gifts they did receive
On the night before when it was Christmas Eve.
There will be all the little girls and all the little boys
Who surely will be playing with all their little toys.

Things have settled down and we offer up a prayer
For giving up His only son for us all to share.
Soon we will all be ushering in the New Year.
Horns will sound and bells will ring for all of us to hear.

It will be noisy and it will be loud.
Many will be going along with the crowd.
They will be standing all along the way
Waiting to hear that it is New Years Day.

Others will be dancing to greet the New Year.
They will whoop it up when it is finally here.
We'll all make resolutions that we intend to keep,
But we'll forget about them when we finally get to sleep.

Christmas Presents or Praises

Each year they start earlier with Christmas ads
Suggesting what to give our mothers and dads
And all the rest of our families and friends.
The selling and buying of gifts never ends.

It does seem to add to the festive air
And people do act like they really care.
Giving gifts is all right in moderation,
But too many gifts is a great temptation.

Commercial aspects of Christmas takes away
From the reason we celebrate Christmas day—
The birth of the Christ child on that special day,
Born in a stable on a bed of hay.

Wrapped in swaddling clothes He received the royalty.
The kings and wisemen came to show their loyalty
Bringing gifts to honor Him and to praise His name,
And following the star the shepherds also came.

We thank God for the gift He has given us all
And we praise the name whenever we recall
The name of Jesus, who taught us how to pray,
Who died that our sins would be taken away.

The Last Minute Gift

'Twas the week before Christmas and all over town
Shoppers were busy rushing around.
There wasn't much left to choose from, you see,
But that last minute gift just had to be

Right for the one it was intended for.
So they were shopping from store to store.
As the day went on they were getting weary
And the weather was getting damp and dreary.

The importance of this gift seemed to get lost.
What they had looked at wasn't worth what it cost.
They decided to pick up something along the way
And be satisfied to just call it a day.

The Feeling of Christmas

A spiritual uplift at the Christmas season,
The birth of the Christ child is the reason.

We get a letdown feeling when it is past
And we are once again ourselves at last.

It's a kind of tired feeling, but it won't be with us long,
For our belief and our faith are very, very strong.

The Spirit of Christmas

It's the time for Christmas holly.
It is the time to be jolly,
For fancy wreaths and mistletoe
And the homes with lights aglow.

Time for people to come calling
While the snow is gently falling.
Some will come their present to bring
And the carolers will come to sing.

Greeting people along the way,
Bringing the spirit of the day
To each home where they are singing.
In the distance bells are ringing.

Celebrating the birth of Jesus,
Showing to all that it pleases
All who know Him and honor His name.
For to die for our sins is why He came.

Christmas Time

Peace on Earth
Good Will Toward Men—
We hear it at Christmas time
But don't hear it again.

Hark the Herald Angels Sing
Is a beautiful song.
We hear it at Christmas time
But not for very long.

Joy to the World
We all like to hear.
We hear it at Christmas time
But not through the year

O Holy Night
Is always sung a lot.
We hear it at Christmas time.
Then it seems to be forgot.

O Little Town of Bethlehem
Is sung with admiration.
We hear it at Christmas time.
Then it's held in reservation.

Away in the Manger
The Christ child lay.
We hear it at Christmas time,
Then it fades away.

The gift that God has given us
Is the one that we adore.
We praise His name at Christmas time
And forever more.

Christmas

Christmas comes but once a year
And it brings us all good cheer.
There's lots of fun along the way
As we watch the children play.

There's holly and mistletoe everywhere
And it shows that people care.
The shopping's done and cards sent out.
Some think that's what it's all about.

But as we kneel and say a prayer,
We feel the spirit in the air.
It's the spirit of good will,
And we know our Savior is with us still.

Santa Claus

St. Nicholas, as the legend goes,
Brought presents to the ones in need
And gave food to the destitute
Who had families to feed.

A tradition started long ago
Giving gifts for a worthy cause
Then as the many years went by
St. Nicholas became Santa Claus.

There is one thing about Santa Claus
That the children should be taught,
Santa Claus brings them one present
And the rest of them are bought.

One present should be left unwrapped
To show that Santa Claus was here.
The milk and cookies left for him
They must somehow disappear.

Yes there is a Santa Claus.
He is the spirit of good will,
Bringing happiness and joy
From our Savior Who is with us still.

New Year's Day

How to welcome in a New Year
Some will raise their glass and cheer.
Each will welcome it in their own way.
There are some who will kneel and pray.

Some go to church on New Years Eve
To thank the Lord for what they receive.
Some make promises they wish to keep.
Others will simply go to sleep.

Some embrace each other and kiss.
They like to celebrate like this.
There are some who will sing and shout.
They think that's what it's all about.

Some will leave when the crowd is gone.
Others will stay until the dawn.
Some will dance the night away
To celebrate this New Years Day.

We each should be a real go-getter
And try to make this New Year better.
The thing that makes a New Year new
Is not what we say but what we do.

Philosophy

Life's Mystery

Life is not as bad as it seems,
But it's not like in our dreams.
Life is full of mystery.
That's the way it was meant to be.

We shouldn't know what lies ahead.
We should keep on going instead.
When we think the road's too rough,
And we think we've had enough,

We mustn't think that we should quit,
For that is the thing of it.
Once we make it up this hill,
We see that there's another still.

Life is based on love thy neighbor,
So we must watch our behavior.
Life is meant to be for giving.
It's a reason for our living.

We must do our very best,
For life is really just a test.
Those who don't understand life's ways
Will surely have some restless days.

God's Plan

The years will come and go and friends will pass away,
And we wonder why it is that we're still here today.
Faith comes by hearing the word and not by seeing.
God is spiritual and we are mortal beings.

He comes to dwell among us in the spirit still,
And keeps us here on earth to carry out His will.
God has a plan for each of us that He'll let us know
While we are still living down here on earth below.

He wants each of us to do good things for others,
Just like they were our sisters and our brothers.
For each one of us great things He is making,
And they are meant to be ours for the taking.

But life is not just taking. There is much to do—
So much to be accomplished before we are through.
God gives special talent for each of us to share
So we may be able to help someone somewhere

To realize God has taken their sin away
When Jesus suffered and died on the cross that day.

The Sacrifice

There were nail holes in His hands.
His feet were that way too.
There was a hole in His side
Where a soldier's spear went through.

His brow was pierced with thorns
From the wreath upon His head
And there He hung before them
Till they pronounced Him dead.

No one but Christ could stand
The suffering and pain
And still be able
To come back to life again.

It was God's love for man
The price that Jesus paid.
A ransom for our sin
Was the sacrifice He made.

His triumph over death
Was meant to show the way
That we can do the same
Even to this day.

His life is everlasting.
Ours can be that way too
If only we believe
That what He did is true.

So when you hear God calling,
You should heed His call.
No matter how much you have sinned,
He will forgive them all.

The Ascension

Following on the heels of his sacrifice
He arose and was with his disciples thrice.
He had made a promise to return again
But no one really believed him then.

Now as they listened to the Savior's voice
The disciples knew that they had no choice.
They must heed his call to teach other men
So they too might become disciples then.

He promised them power from the Holy Ghost
And they would be witnesses from coast to coast.
They received the Spirit on Pentecost day
And each understood what the others would say.

The disciples were able to see him leave
And when Christ saw they were starting to grieve
He spoke to them in a very soft manner
"Take up my staff and carry my banner."

When the transfiguration had taken place
Very few people had seen Jesus' face.
I go to prepare a place for you
So where I am you will be there too.

A comforter will be sent in my name
The Holy Ghost is the one that came.
Father Son and Holy Ghost is the Trinity
Which is the foundation of our Divinity.

So that you may eternal life receive
You must repent of your sins and believe.
Receive the Spirit and be born again
Through Jesus the redeemer of men.

Life's Idiosyncrasies

When the usual seems unusual we ask ourselves why,
For we know the reason cannot be because we do not try.
When things keep going wrong for you and you don't know
    what to do,
Take a deep breath and relax for a while and then think it
    through.

We all tend to regiment our lives to live a routine way.
When anything disrupts our routine it ruins our whole day.
Things are always popping up that really throw us a curve.
That's when we need a little fortitude to back up our nerve.

We are aware that into each life a little rain must fall,
But there are times in our lives it seems we are getting it all.
Life is not meant to always run smooth and that we
    understand,
And we know that sometimes we all will need a helping hand.

But it is up to us with a little help from our friends
To see that we are in control by the time each day ends.

The Ebb Tide of Our Life

As we near the ebb tide of our life
And we are growing old and grey,
Just count the blessings that we have
That help to send us on our way.

Little things are important now
That we used to pass right over.
Compared to what we have been through,
We are now knee deep in clover.

Enjoy the good life that we have.
Our life must wane—it is God's plan.
We must live by what He taught us.
He'll judge us on the race we ran.

When we finally fade away
And we tell our final story
In the place He prepared for us,
We will dwell in all its glory.

Losing a Loved One

With the passing of our loved one
Whose been with us all these years,
There's a feeling of emptiness
And we can't hold back our tears.

We know that God will comfort us
If only we believe,
But we know within our heart
The pain will never leave.

They haven't really left us—
They've just gone on ahead
To the place prepared for them,
Just as Jesus said.

Each time that we remember them
There's a sadness in our heart
And the lonesomeness returns
Because we are apart.

Tears for a Loved One

Losing a loved one is harder than before.
It's surely not because we have loved them more.
As we age we get more sentimental.
This could be the thing that is instrumental.

In making it so much harder to bear
By helping us realize how much we care.
It's hard to accept kind words from others.
It's also hard for our sisters and brothers.

One can't escape from the hurt it causes
And at the gravesite as each friend pauses
It brings back memories of other years,
And with those memories it brings us tears

With a feeling of sadness and remorse.
So crying becomes our only recourse.

Beginning Life Anew

Once the one you love is gone,
Your own life must still go on.
You must lift your chin and bear it.
Now you have no one to share it.

Death is not grim as we've been told.
It's just a part of growing old.
God will help you find a way
To make it through from day to day.

Cherish the memories you hold
Of the things that you've been told.
Your children now must be a part
Of the new life that you must start.

Memories

A sigh quickly dissipates into the air.
A kiss impresses but for the moment.
A strand which has come from her lovely hair.

All these are things which our dreams are made of.
We try to overlook them but to no avail,
For sometimes we confuse them with real love.

In time these memories will dim and fade away.
We must renew the feelings that we have had
And do it consistently from day to day.

The Easy Way

The things we cherish most sometimes
Are the things that we forget—
To say "hello" and give a smile
And say "I'm glad we met."

To greet the family members
And say "Please," "Thank you" and "Hi,"
To wish them well as they depart
And say to them "Goodbye."

How about our friends,
Do we neglect them too?
How many of them are there
That our letters are past due?

We think about these things
And think that's the way to go.
But when the day is over,
There is nothing there to show.

It's so easy to put things off
And take the easy way.
But with just a little effort,
We could do these things today.

Learning

When I was a little child I used to wonder why
I couldn't do what grownups did no matter how I'd try.
As I got a little older I was full of questions then
That all needed answers as to Who What Why and When.

Then came the teenage years when there was nothing more to
    learn.
But when something would go wrong, to whom was I to turn?
In my twenties the questions started all over again
And it seemed a bigger problem to find the answers then.

Then when I got married everything was all so new
I didn't know what I should say or what I was to do.
There was so much about marriage that I didn't know.
It was like a learning course as through the years I'd go.

Then there were the children I must be a parent too.
We had to help each other. There was too much for one to do.
When I reached my senior years I still wonder a lot
About the things that I should know but I was never taught.

Take It Easy

As you get older
You will get bolder
And do things you shouldn't do.
So slow down a bit
Before it's too late
And something happens to you.

You've lived your spring
And summer years
So now you're in early fall.
It's better to do
A little bit
Than to do nothing at all.

We're all so busy
We fail to see
The things that life discloses.
Sometime each day
All of us should
Take time to smell the roses.

So take it easy
And you will find
That life will be fuller then.
It's nice to have
Such friends as you
To think of now and again.

Be Prepared

When you go to sleep never to awaken,
Never feel that you will ever be forsaken.
Death is not the grim reaper as we have been told.
It is a natural process of growing old.

God has control of the way, the time and the place,
So we must always be ready just in case.
Since God is the only one who knows our fate,
If we're not ready when He comes it will be too late.

By confessing our sins and become born again,
We'll be prepared for His coming no matter when.

The Good Old Days

There's the good old days
And the modern ways.
They seem so far apart.
We'd like to close
The gap between
But don't know where to start.

There is good and bad
In each of them
So they're not out of reach.
It seems there ought
To be some way
That we could close the breach.

There is really not
Much difference
Between the old and new.
It's mostly in
The way we talk
And in the things we do.

There's a difference in
The clothes we wear.
The styles have changed a lot.
What we used to
Make ourselves
Are mostly now store bought.

Neither are likely
To ever change
So it'll go on as before.
Each one thinking
Their way is the best
And they can offer more.

As we grow older
Some will yearn
For the good old days.
I don't know about
The rest of you
But I'll take the modern ways.

Too Old?

Don't ever say that you're too old.
You might begin to think it's true.
Think of the memories you hold
And all the things you used to do.

You've past the age of no return
And you have sat and reflected.
That should give you some concern
For some things make you feel dejected.

If you aren't the one selected
And you think it's time for quitting,
If you feel that you're neglected
Then you'll find you'll just be sitting.

So you just sit and start to worry
And feel life holds no more for you.
While life passes in a hurry
That is when you're really through.

I'll bet you know a lot of things—
Things you like to say and do—
That others would find interesting
And if you share them, so would you.

So go out where you are needed.
They're just like you—they need a friend.
And after you have succeeded,
You'll find that it is not the end.

A Helping Hand

When you're on your own
And you're all alone
And don't know where to go
You walk the street
And those you meet
Are no one that you know.

You look around
And think you found
A place for you to stay.
When you get there
You are made aware
That this is not your day.

The rent's too high
For you to try
For you're not working yet.
You fill the applications
But they all have reservations
And jobs are pretty hard to get.

You think of the "Y"
But walk right on by—
It's not what you had in mind.
You need a bed
To lay your head
But you want the best you can find.

You hear a sound
And you look around—
It's the Salvation Army band
Now things look bright
And it seems all right
For they lend you a helping hand.

Now things are better.
You write them a letter
And thank them for helping you out.
Now you realize
To your surprise
That's what they're all about.

You drop in now and then
To thank them again
For you have been made aware
When you run out of time
And you've spent your last dime,
There are people who really care.

The Grass Is Always Greener

The neighbors move out
With their dogs and cats.
New neighbors move in,
Now we have mice and rats.

We complain about neighbors
And about their lawn,
But we sure miss them
When they are gone.

How they live
Is no business of ours.
We think about this
As we enjoy their flowers.

We leave our town
Because the pay is higher,
But before very long
We lose our desire.

Money doesn't seem
So important as then,
And we'd like to return
Back home again.

We're homesick now
For the things that we
Remember the way
Things used to be.

The grass is not greener—
It just seems that way.
We're back home again,
This time to stay.

Money will never
Replace a friend,
And that is the way
This story should end.

Wishing

If wishes were horses then beggars would ride
And we'd wish for something in which we'd take pride.
Wishing is something that all people do
And you will find that it's not something new.

We've all been wishing since we were a child.
Some of our wishes have been pretty wild.
Starlight, starbright, first star I've seen tonight.
I wish I may I wish I might get the wish I wish tonight.

Just one of our wishes as a child we make,
We wish when blowing candles on our birthday cake.
We're pulling the wishbone, our wish to ensure,
A tradition it seems will always endure.

We wish good fortune for all of our friends
And we wish that our friendship never ends.
The wishing well has always been part of our lives.
It's another tradition that we hope survives.

We wish for the good times and strive to achieve
The things that we want and what we believe.
We wish our children would have the desire
For as much education as they can acquire.

Craving is wishing, it's all the same,
And wishing is really kind of a game.
We crave the food and don't hesitate
Though we know it will put on more weight.

We diet and exercise to make ourselves thin,
Yet we know from the start that we cannot win.
We need a genie to grant us our wishes
But that doesn't mean that we're superstitious.

Some say wishing is dreaming and that may be true,
But without dreaming what would we do?
Dreaming is how we get our inventions,
So we must dream with the best of intentions.

Emotions

Happiness and sadness both come from the heart.
We must learn to separate and keep them apart
To show each emotion one by one.
Although it's not easy, it must be done.

There's a very fine line between sad and glad.
We shed tears when we're happy and tears when we're sad.
Emotions range from high to low progressively.
Sometimes it seems that they do it excessively.

From love to wonder
From wonder to doubt
From doubt to worry
From worry to fear
From fear to despair
From despair to suicide.

Love

There are many kinds of love
That we can show each other,
Like the love we have
For our sister and our brother.

There's the puppy love we had
When we were very young.
It seemed to be so real
When all was said and done.

There's the love we show
For all the family pets
And the love they show
For the attention that each gets.

We fall in love with teachers
But they are unaware,
But they do not return our love
For they don't know it's there.

Then there is the special love
That we know is real,
And we tell the other folks
So they'll know how we feel.

So on our wedding day
We have mixed emotions,
But we both exchange
Our love and our devotions.

There are many kinds of love
We experience in life,
But there's no love as great
As the love we show our wife.

There's a new kind of love
When our babies arrive.
It makes us feel that
We are more alive.

There's the love we have
For our children's achievement
And the family's love
In times of bereavement.

There's the love we have
That we hold within
For the Christ our Savior
Who died for our sin.

Pride

Take pride in your achievements
And in your children too.
Be proud of the place you work
And of what your children do.

Be proud of your country's flag
And of what it represents.
Take pride in the way you live
And of other's compliments.

Pride is a wonderful thing to have
If we don't abuse it.
But if it makes us all puffed up,
That's when we misuse it.

Take pride in our church and schools
But don't be vain about it.
Vanity is worshiping another God
So we must do without it.

Don't be boastful about your possessions.
After all is said and done,
It's another form of worship,
But we can only worship One.

Frustration

If you find yourself wrestling with your conscience
And you are not able to sleep at night,
Things don't seem to be like they were before
And you don't know what is causing this plight,

Your nerves seem to be almost ready to snap
And you can't see the forest for the trees,
But you still don't know what is making it so,
You should back up and put yourself at ease.

You'll have to find what is causing it all
And a way to solve the problems you meet.
There surely must be something someone can do
And the help you need to get back on your feet.

So try to relax and take it easy.
Talk to the family or even a friend.
It just might ease your conscience a little
And bring your frustration to an end.

Sympathy?

Sympathy you want, sympathy you get.
You're not able to come home yet?
You lie in bed until you ache.
Come on get up for goodness sake.

You lie in bed like you are ill
And they'll give you another pill.
You wonder if you're really missed.
We'll tell you yes if you insist.

You'll be glad when you are able
To again sit at the table.
Better yet we will be lookin'
For the day when you start cookin'.

You're anxious to go home I'll bet.
You're not able to go home yet.
Wait until they tell you "Now."
Your folks will get along somehow.

The Process of Divorce

When our love is new
Things we say and do
Make up our wonderful love.
Seems the more we know
Helps our love to grow
And we know it comes from above.

Our love should last
As the years go past.
We're happy as we can be.
As we go hand in hand
Knowing our love will stand
For no one's in love as we.

But in each our life
Comes the stress and strife
And we start drifting apart.
As we start to doubt
What it's all about,
It seems that we've just lost heart.

It is just too bad
And it's all too sad
For it's not what our marriage intended.
As we each go our way
There is no more to say,
For now our marriage has ended.

Stress and Strife

Your house is tacky
And you're going wacky
And you think you'll lose your mind.
Your boss at work
Is such a jerk
For he is one of a kind.

You work all day
And then you say
"I'm never going to get through."
They bring you more
And you get sore.
It's starting to get to you.

You start to shout
Then you walk out
And you feel like this is the end.
It makes you weep
And you can't sleep
So your resignation you send.

You find work near home
Where you're free to roam
And you have some time to have fun.
You find things that you
Always wanted to do
And now you can get them done.

Now your house is neat
And you're not all beat.
You spend time with your family.
There's more to life
Than stress and strife
And life is like it ought to be.

Sleepless Nights

Sleep just seems to hesitate
So we just close our eyes and wait.
We toss and turn in our bed
And thoughts keep running through our head.

We think of things we need to do
And other things we think of too.
When we lay awake and think,
Maybe all we need's a drink.

Maybe if we have some food
It would put us in the mood.
To the bathroom to ponder our plight
Why it is we can't sleep at night.

We hope sleep comes before daylight
For we haven't slept all night.
There's medicine for us to take
That makes us sleep when we're awake.

But I would rather lose the sleep.
The pills I'd rather that they keep.
They will only make you drowsy
Also make you feel real lousy.

When we wake up at the dawn,
All we want to do is yawn.
Our body's tired and our brain too.
We feel this way the whole day through.

We get sleepy during the day
And we doze the day away.
We miss the programs on T.V.
Our eyelids close and we can't see.

When we can't get the sleep we yearn
I guess we should have some concern.
To the doctor we should go.
If something's wrong it might not show.

World Problems

Take the world's problems off your shoulder
For you will find as you grow older
Those kind of problems won't go away.
They are the kind that are here to stay.

Fighting, corruption, greed and crime
Have been with us all of the time.
Murder, rape, prostitution and drugs—
These are all operated by thugs.

Syndicates control the action
And must meet their satisfaction.
There will always be wars someplace
So nations prepare just in case.

The weapons they use are better now—
As powerful as the laws allow.
No matter how much food we send
Starvation round the world won't end.

So you see there is no ending
And there is no use pretending.
That is the reason that I say
All these problems are here to stay.

The Solution

Busy hands and busy feet
Keep the children off the street.
The more you study the more you learn
So when you work the more you'll earn.

If I am not in the mood
For a certain kind of food,
If I shouldn't really care
For the clothes I have to wear,

If I turn and look around
And don't like the things I've found,
If I'm not in a hurry
And I don't have a worry,

It must be because I'm bored
Or losing sleep I can't afford.
Now there must be a solution
To enrich my constitution.

To rid the feeling of duress
I might help those in distress.
It's an age-old cure for most ills
And it's much better than taking pills.

Why Was I Born

Have you ever awakened one morn
And asked yourself why was I born?
What is my purpose here on earth?
Am I working for all I am worth?

Am I fulfilling my daily task,
Doing whatever others ask,
Seeking people who need my aid,
Correcting mistakes that I have made?

Everyone has a special calling.
Perhaps to keep someone from falling,
Perhaps to save a drowning man
Or help someone when no one else can.

To help someone across the street
Or extend a hand to those we meet.
I believe we're to help each other
Like they were our sister or brother.

Promises

PROMISE: An oral or written agreement to do or not to do something. A vow, to give a basis for expectation. To pledge, to assure, to declare emphatically.

Promises to keep, promises to break,
Promises should be kept for others' sake.
Broken promises could be tragic
For children who believe in magic.

Little white lies are lies just the same—
A broken promise by another name.
A pledge made should never be broken.
It is more than a few words spoken.

Tongue in cheek promises are not real.
Imagine how those, they're made to feel.
Fingers crossed promises made as a joke
Are made in fun and meant to be broke.

Guarantees are promises of a kind
And most will be honored one will find.
A man's word given was as good as gold.
A handshake was a contract I am told.

Resolutions are made with high hope
For problems which one just cannot cope.
A solemn promise is a vow
That is forever—not just for now.

Promise a basis for expectation
Is believed without hesitation
When it is made known one's intention
It should be done without intervention.

When all parties finally agree
A declaration of what it will be
Is signed by all parties as good will
So years from now it will be good still.

There are lots of promises one might use.
It's up to each which one they will choose.
Those for convenience, the brush off kind,
Or those that are intended to bind.

Habits

We are creatures of habit one might say
As we do the same things day after day.
Habits are formed when we are very small
As we grow older we don't keep them all.

Our habits change as we grow older.
As we age we will get much bolder
And we experiment with new things.
We change our lifestyle as each year brings

New Challenges—new thoughts—new ideas
And new desires which might free us
From the daily regimentation
Of our habit forming creation.

About mid-life we feel ourselves slip.
Old habits have us back in their grip.
It is hard to shake our old habits when
They keep coming back again and again.

So we give up and think what is the use.
To ease our conscience we give some excuse.
Habits are stronger than the will of man.
To break them I doubt if anyone can.

Monotony

If things don't go the way you have them planned
Then you must back off and take a different stand.
Interruptions help to avoid monotony
And that is the way that life ought to be.

Think how dull life would be without adversities
And none of us would have responsibilities.
From time to time we must enjoy life's treasures.
Life holds a goodly store, just for our pleasures.

This helps relieve the monotony of life
And thus eliminates the stress and strife.
Routine is different than monotony.
It's regimentation of our life, you see.

Monotony is sort of like counting sheep.
It's something we could almost do in our sleep.
Don't let monotony get the best of you.
If it's that routine, find something else to do.

Cliches

Cliches are sayings handed down through the ages,
And there still is some good advice on these pages.

"Smile and the world smiles with you"
Is it real or just a cliche?
Try it sometime and you will find
Others will do it your way.

"Weep and you weep alone"
Is one of another dimension.
Try it sometime and you will find
It surely does get their attention.

"The way to make an enemy is loan money to a friend"
It works out for a little while,
But you'll lose them in the end.

"A penny saved is a penny earned"
A cliche that we should heed
For there will come a time you know
When they will fill our need.

"Take care of your pennies and your dollars
will take care of themselves"
A very sound business principle that helps
To fill up your shelves.

"A stitch in time saves nine"
That's the way the saying goes.
It helps to lighten up our load
Of torn and tattered clothes.

"The way to a man's heart is through his stomach"
you've heard some people say
But it seems to work out very well even to this day.

"Honesty is the best policy"
So don't tell the first lie,
Then you don't have to keep adding them just to get by.

"He who hesitates is lost"
So we must change our thinking.
If we don't, then we might find that our ship is sinking.

"A bird in the hand is worth two in the bush"
So stop reaching for the rest
For that which you already have you'll find to be the best.

"He who laughs last laughs best"
So don't laugh at another's boo boo.
Just remember the very same thing could also happen to you.

"If March comes in like a lamb, it goes out like a lion
and visa versa" it's true,
So pay attention and watch the weather
So it doesn't sneak up on you.

"April showers bring May flowers"
As everyone should know.
So welcome the rains and hope they come
So the flowers will grow.

"You can't have your cake and eat it too"
For when you eat it you're all through.
Between what you want and what you want to do,
You must make a choice—it's up to you.

"Eat what you can and what you can't, can"
No one is sure where this saying began.

"All that glitters is not gold"
Is more truth than fiction I've been told.
So watch that you don't get mistreated
And beware so you don't get cheated.

"Never look a gift horse in the mouth"
For you don't know what you would find.
It could be either good or bad so thank
The giver for being so kind.

"Where there is a will there is a way"
We have heard other people say.
There is no problem that can't be solved
If all of us will get involved.

"Don't count your chickens before they hatch"
For you may have a bad batch,
Then you will never know for sure just how many will hatch.

"Make hay while the sun shines"
Is a saying that is true.
If the hay should get wet, you'll find it will mildew.

"There's more than one way to skin a cat"
I think I'll just let it go at that.

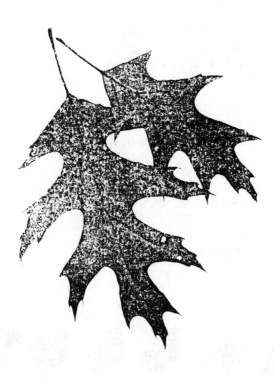

Nature

Why the Seasons?

If the flowers bloom in May
As I have heard some people say,
What then can be the reason
That we have the other seasons?

Is it just for variation
Of the other vegetation—
The change of color Fall will bring
And changing back again in Spring?

With the winter sandwiched in between,
When there is no sign of green
With all the leaves gone from the trees
And the snow up to your knees.

A respite from the bugs and things
And the insects that bite and stings,
It really does make one wonder
Did Mother Nature make a blunder?

When we stop and think about it,
We would surely have to doubt it.
There has to be a real good reason
For the changing of the seasons.

God has charge of all these things.
That must be why each quarter brings
A change of Nature all around
So the beauty of each will abound.

Sights and Sounds of Spring

The storms and chill to winter cling
But then relent and bring us spring.
The long awaited time is here—
The time of splendor for each year.

The stirring of the plants and things
Brings us the sights and sounds of spring.
The breeze is softer now and still
The air retains the winter's chill.

But now the birds are on the wing
To bring us sights and sounds of spring,
And they feel that they must sing
To let us know that it is spring.

It's time to plow the ground asunder
For we have heard the clap of thunder,
To turn the soil and pull the weeds
Where we intend to plant our seeds.

Prepare the soil in advance
Where we intend to set our plants.
Although the work seems awfully hard,
We still must clean up all the yard.

And to us thus the rain will bring
The many sights and sounds of spring.
The planting of the crops will bear
Enough for all of us to share.

So gather now that we may sing
And heed the sights and sounds of spring.
Spring is a busy time of year,
But aren't you glad that it is here?

When the Robins Return

When the robins return each year,
Then we know that spring is here.
First there will be just a few,
Then more will come to join them too.

We see them hopping all around,
Looking for worms beneath the ground.
As they hop across the yard
They find it's still a bit too hard.

They're persistent and patient too.
They will find some before they're through.
When they do pull up a worm,
You can see the poor thing squirm.

But that's what keeps robins alive
So they are able to survive.
Their cheerful chirp and hopping way—
Just watching them will make your day.

They'll choose a place to build their nest
Then let nature do the rest.
Now they are busy hunting food
So they can feed their hungry brood.

They never do need any care
Just so they find water there.
They're such a pleasure when they're here.
We hope they'll come back every year.

The Robins

Two robins in an apple tree—
One for you and one for me.
They fly around because they're free—
One for you and one for me.

When they fly, they sing with glee—
One for you and one for me.
They build a nest for their family
'Cause one's a He and the other a She.

When the Lilacs Bloom

When the lilacs bloom in May
We're happy for we know that they
Indicate that spring is here
And summertime is very near.

Lilacs of many colors grow,
Which of course most of us know,
White, pink, red, purple and blue,
A bluish-red called lilac too.

It is kind of hard to choose
The color that you want to use.
The clusters do make nice bouquets,
And they last for several days.

The scent from the lilac's bloom
Will waft across and fill the room.
The pleasure that the lilacs bring
We treasure more than anything.

We must keep the plants alive
So the blossoms will survive.
They really don't require much care.
They will grow most anywhere.

So the blooms we love so much
Give our yard a majestic touch,
And the blooms will have a place
In a room within a vase.

Vegetation

From the mighty oaks to the redwood trees,
Reaching for the sun as they sway in the breeze,
From a blade of grass to the lowly weed,
All get their start from a tiny seed.

The seed dropped or planted will grow just the same.
It's up to the planters to give them a name.
Once they are started, nature does the rest—
Feeding and watering so they'll be their best.

The culturists strive to improve the strain
So it will be different from the main.
Some plants are cultured to use for show.
Others are grafted so they will grow

Different species from the same limb
And still keep the plant or tree fit and trim.
From the smallest plant to a tree out of reach—
It is God's plan to produce some of each.

Some will die out to meet the need,
For only the strongest to succeed.

Speaking of the Weather

Speaking of the weather,
Which most people do
When they get together
And the skies are blue,

It's beautiful to see
When the sun shines bright
And most folks will agree
It gives them great delight.

When all the flowers have bloomed
And all the grass is green,
The yards have just been groomed
As pretty as you've seen.

What is this that's taking place?
It's too early yet for fall.
Maybe it is just one case
And won't affect them all.

The flowers are drooping down
And the leaves are dropping.
The grass is turning brown
And there seems to be no stopping.

It's a quirk of nature
And it is called a drought—
Something we do not savor
And we could do without.

We know that without the rain
The crops will surely die.
We pray God will come again
And open up the sky.

It is the only way
To keep the crops alive,
So we must kneel and pray
So others may survive.

Speaking of the weather,
Here's what most people say
When they get together
And the skies are gray.

It seems God has heard our prayers.
He will answer them somehow.
Though we hear thunder upstairs,
It might not be right now.

If we're patient and believe,
I am sure without a doubt
The rains we will receive
And they will end the drought.

Since this has happened before
And we have weathered it through,
Some of us should know the score
And know just what to do.

Cut down on the water we use.
No watering of the lawn.
The dying grass is no excuse
Or all our water will be gone.

Summertime

Now as we bid farewell to spring,
We get insects that bite and sting.
The work of spring is almost done.
It's time to be out in the sun,

Or in the shade to keep us cool,
Or go swimming in a pool,
To work or play as we desire,
Or sit and dream what we aspire.

There's lots of things that we should do.
No matter what, we're never through.
The weeds are getting mighty thick,
And there they stand for us to pick.

We should do something that is fun
Instead of lying in the sun.
Vacation time is drawing near.
What will we plan to do this year?

Maybe we could go someplace.
We should pack if that's the case.
Our travel plans have gone astray—
Too much to do to get away.

Summer's great if we can take it,
But I guess it's what we make it.
It might be an exciting summer
Or it could be just another bummer.

Summer Evenings

In the evening when the shadows grow long
And the birds are singing their favorite song
You will see folks leisurely walking the street
Pausing to greet other folks that they meet.

People sitting on porches along the way
At the end of another busy day
Waving a greeting to those passing by
Then brushing away an occasional fly.

Families going for a bicycle ride.
They are all in a line and not side by side.
Older children first then younger ones you'll find.
To watch the children the parents ride behind.

The more ambitious folks playing croquet
And badminton too some folks like to play.
Hide and go seek is a popular game
For children who find the others too tame.

People differ in things they like to do
Swimming, boating, golfing to name a few.
Some stay home and take care of their flowers.
Some just sit and relax a few hours.

Summer evenings are a boon to mankind.
No other time is as pleasant you'll find.
We bask in the beauty of twilight's glow
Until darkness of night begins to show.

What A Sight

You watch the lights growing dimmer by the evening glow
And you think to yourself of course, "what a show—
      what a show."
Now the evening glow blends in with the darkness of night
And you think to yourself again, "what a sight—
      what a sight."

Late into the night you watch the lights constantly changing
And each time you look they seem to still be rearranging.
You wonder if this could be an optical illusion.
Then you wonder what causes you to come to this conclusion.

The lights of course remain the same—they just appear to
      change.
The atmospheric condition makes them seem to rearrange.
Now you turn your attention to the stars in the sky
And you think what an awesome sight as they go sailing by.

You get the feeling this must be the all-time show of shows,
For what you watched on earth can't compare as the saying
      goes.
The celestial patterns are so hard to discern
The vastness of the stars makes it hard for one to learn.

Countless stars keep falling and there are more that take their
      place.
It is hard to comprehend what takes place in
      outer space.
The awesomeness engulfs you like a shroud around your being
And it is hard to really understand what you are seeing.

As you watch, the time slips away until it is daylight
And you think to yourself once more, "what a sight— what a
      sight."

A Tiny Nook

Near glassy waters of a brook
The grassy banks form a tiny nook
A tranquil place where one can find
Peace for both their soul and mind.

Where one can leave their cares behind
And ease the tension of their mind
Then sit and dream of long ago
And watch the sparkling water flow.

As they gaze into the brook
They recall pictures that they took
Of places similar to this
Where one could find this kind of bliss.

A sanctuary where one could be
Alone with their thoughts and be free
From all the worldly rush and din
Where one could find their rest within.

They come back time and time again.
It is refreshing to them when
They receive a Spiritual lift
From Mother Nature as a gift.

The Heat of Summer

The heat of the summer air makes it unbearable to sleep.
We take our quilts out on the lawn and then try counting
    sheep.
But no matter what we try, the heat is too much to bear.
We even try using a fan to circulate the air.

It seems to help a little bit but doesn't do it all,
So we ask the air conditioning people to come and install
A unit in the home that will be able to cool the air
So we can live in comfort in our home almost anywhere.

Where Did Our Summer Go

What happened to our summer?
From whence comes this cool air?
Did summer really leave us
While we were unaware?

The trees, grass and shubbery
Still retain the summer's green.
If it continues, autumn
Will be the earliest we've seen.

I don't think I'm quite ready
To give up our summer yet.
I'll just put on a few more clothes
And take all the sun I can get.

Nature plays these little pranks
At least once or twice each year
So we will appreciate
What we have while it is here.

The Beauty of Fall

When we leave the busy highways
And drive along the country by-ways,
The beauty of the fall abounds
As nature changes all around.

The changing color of the trees,
Leaves that are falling in the breeze,
Some things to see along the way,
Are all the fields of new mown hay.

The farmers taking in the grain
Make haste to finish 'fore the rain.
They reap the harvest of the fall
So there's plenty of work for all.

So much to do before the frost—
Pick all the fruit so it's not lost.
Now it's time to prepare the meat
For the winter for them to eat.

Some feel hard work is their duty
So they fail to see the beauty.
Mend the fence and repair the shed—
These are jobs they always dread.

Paint the buildings so they glisten—
These are things for all who listen
For howling winds that bring the snow.
Where did all our summer go?

Nature's Way

Once again I am watching the changing of color
That ushers in the fall.
This is a natural process which takes place
Each year at this time when all

The trees and plants and all the foliage
Sheds its green summer attire
And takes on the yellows, oranges, reds,
And browns that we so much admire.

Since foliage does not all change at the same time,
Its beauty is extended,
And we are able to enjoy it
Until all the process has ended.

God's paint brush does its work
In spring and in early fall,
And the wonder of its magic
Is a joy to one and all.

The Fox Hunt

They wait until the clarion sounds
Then they mount and release the hounds.
They start out at a leisurely pace,
Then they all join in the chase.

Each relies on their trusty steed
As each one tries to gain the lead.
They jump the fences along the way
While the hounds hold the fox at bay.

Now another clarion sounds
To end the hunt and call off the hounds.
The fox is captured and put away
To be used again another day.

The valets care for all the steeds.
The riders tend to their own needs
And discuss the day's event
And how the ride of each one went.

The fox hunt is a social affair
So the elite are always there.
It's the last outdoor event of fall
So it will bid farewell to all.

The Chill of Winter

As the icy winds begin to blow,
It reminds us of the snow
We had forgotten in other seasons.
And no matter what the reasons,

It ushers in the winter chill,
And we know it is the will
Of Mother Nature's final play
To end the seasons in her way.

The earth is blanketed with snow
To give a place for those to go
Who like to play in snow and ski.
But there are those who are like me

Who like to stay in by the fire
And do the things that they admire.
There's less to do and more time to spend
To read or play or clothes to mend.

But when the holidays are here
We wish that all our friends were near
So together we could share
The Christmas spirit in the air.

The sparkling of new fallen snow
Gives it a special kind of glow
Which helps us while we wait until
The ending of the winter's chill.

One Wintry Night

All is still on this wintry night but the
Sound of the howling wind,
The crackling sound of the roaring fire and
The tick of the clock within.

The silence is broken with the tinkling of
Sleigh bells from across the way
As the hardy folks brave the winter chill
To come out and drive their sleigh.

The scent of popcorn in the room seems to
Accent the winter air.
The feeling of winter seems to be coming
From almost everywhere.

While the flames from some of the hearth
Fire logs are still burning low,
Other logs where the flames have gone
Out still remain aglow.

The evening has nearly slipped away and
It is almost bed time.
The grandfather clock in the hall is
Just about ready to chime.

It has been an enjoyable evening despite
The winter chill
Now that the noise has all subsided and
Once again all is still.

We should be able to soundly sleep all
The way through this night
And not be bothered with any noise until
It is daylight.

Snowflakes

As the flakes fall softly down to the ground,
They float and they tumble without any sound.
We gaze and we wonder from where they came.
We notice that there are no two the same.

We feel they are one of God's greatest creation,
And so we watch them with great admiration.
A breeze starts to stir and blows them away,
And we realize that they are not here to stay.

As the breeze turns to wind it becomes much stronger,
And we wish to ourselves they would be around longer.
Now the wind driven flakes begin to start sifting.
As the snow flakes pile up, this causes the drifting.

The roads are all filling with new fallen snow.
It's drifting so high we're unable to go.
We get out our shovels, our blades and our blowers.
Not long ago we had out our mowers.

What started to be one of nature's great wonders
Has turned out to be one of nature's great blunders.

The Sun

As the sun dispels the dark of night
It brings the rays of day's first light.
The moonlight dims and fades away.
The sun begins another day.

It's one of God's creations too,
So it has a big job to do.
Not just the light that it will bring
and energy to each living thing,

But also heat to warm each day
As it passes along its way.
It seems to race across the sky
Like it hurries to pass us by.

In the evening the twilight glows.
The sun puts on one of its shows.
Next to the sunrise, it's the best.
What a sight to see while we rest

From all the toils of the day
As the sun sets in its usual way.
When the darkness of night surrounds us,
There is something that astounds us.

Another light will be here soon—
The sun's reflection from the moon.
Thus the sun in all its beauty
Never fails to do its duty.

The Voices of Nature's Inanimate World

The mighty roar of an angry ocean
When it is showing its emotion,
The lapping sound when the waves reach the beach,
The water sending the spray out of reach,

The ripples coming from a gentle wave,
The echoes coming from a deep, dark cave,
The clapping thunder from out of the sky,
The howling wind as it goes passing by,

The silence before the tornado hits,
The roaring sound while it tears things to bits,
The creaking, cracking sound when the earth slips,
The similar sound by capsizing ships,

The falling rocks to the highway below
Make loud, crashing sounds wherever they go.
The whirring sound of the shifting sand
As it forms the dunes across the land,

The music coming from out of the trees
When they are swaying from a soft, summer breeze,
The willow is weeping as its branches sway.
We can almost hear what it has to say.

The reeds in the marshlands play night and day.
We hear them when passing along their way.
The whispering sound of the fields of grain,
The pitter-patter of the drops of rain,

The freezing of ice makes a crackling sound,
There are voices of nature all around.
Music is important to nature's plan.
Pictures play their part as nothing else can.

The Dove

It was such an ugly thing when it broke through its shell.
It was checked very carefully to make sure that it was well.
It was bred to be a show bird, right from the start,
And later would be trained, so it could play its part.

As it grew a little older it was found to be all right.
There were no markings on it so it would be all white.
It was destined to perform in a magician's act,
So there was formed between them a special kind of pact.

Through the years they traveled, all throughout the land,
And from time to time the dove would need a helping hand.
Finally came the day the dove would have to go.
It was just too big to keep performing on the show.

What to do with a dove whose use came to an end.
Perhaps it could be given to a special friend.
Now that the dove has been placed in its new home
No more performing, no more having to roam.

Now its new owners must be made aware
The dove with its fine breeding must be given special care.
Its remaining years will be all of its own,
And the best part of all it will not be alone.

It still is entertaining and interesting to see,
But instead of entertaining crowds, it entertains the family.

Fantasy

Reflections

Reflection is the mirror of our life
With all its problems and all its strife.
We try to reflect on things of today,
But it seems that they just slip away.

Into the past our reflections cling
With all the wonders reflections bring
Days of our childhood so long ago,
School days and classmates we used to know.

Reflections keep coming close to each other.
They seem to overlap one another
Reflecting teenage crushes and such,
Proms and parties—it all seemed too much.

The best times of our lives came later on
Just when our good times seemed to be gone.
These reflections though they may come late
Reflect the one we chose as our mate.

As our reflections fade away,
They bring us back to the present day.
We see our reflection once again.
How different our lives are now from then!

A Sentimental Journey

A sentimental journey
Is so fantastic
We don't do anything
That is very drastic.

As we board the memories
That take us back
We know right away
We are on the right track.

There's a mystic feeling
About our yearning
To go back in time
And then returning.

We try to remember
What happened one day
But it burst like a bubble
Then faded away.

As we clear the cobwebs
That cloud up our view
It really does help
To see things anew.

To freshen our memories
Of our wildest schemes
And then bring to mind
Our beautiful dreams.

The things we've seen
And places we've been,
The things we've done
We remember again.

Friends we've forgotten
Come back to mind
And that is a wonderful
Treasure to find.

When we get back
To when we were kids,
The things we said
And the things we did

Are priceless memories
To have and to hold
Through our later years
When we are growing old.

We drink in the visions
From out of the past.
We never know how long
These journeys will last.

We just went for a visit.
We didn't intend to stay.
We can't compare the past
With what it's like today.

The Pages of Time

Turning back the pages of time
Is not an easy thing to do.
When we try to turn them one by one,
They stick together like glue.

We try to pull the pages apart
To see what they hold inside,
But they simply will not open up
No matter how hard we tried.

The only way to turn them back
Is to get the old gang together.
But they have all scattered about
Like a shipwreck in stormy weather.

How can we contact one of them?
Maybe we'll send them a letter.
A phone call or a telegram
Might be even better.

That might not be so easy.
The years have gone by so fast.
They might not even remember
That they were once in our past.

An ad in our home town paper
For someone to contact us,
It might just bring us good results
And save us a lot of fuss.

It is real important now
That we open up our past.
Our future is not important.
Our memories are what last.

If we cannot open it all,
We might have to settle for less.
What we cannot remember,
We will simply have to guess.

This Dreamy Wonderland of Love

In this dreamy dreamy wonderland of love
There is the wonder of anticipation
And the ecstasy of realization,
In this dreamy dreamy wonderland of love.

In this dreamy dreamy wonderland of love,
When two people in love whose hearts beat as one,
There's a mystic feeling nothing can be done,
In this dreamy dreamy wonderland of love.

In this dreamy dreamy wonderland of love
There's the feeling of delight in what they do,
For to them companionship is something new,
In this dreamy dreamy wonderland of love.

In this dreamy dreamy wonderland of love,
Now the two of them are learning to see
What lifelong friendship together could be,
In this dreamy dreamy wonderland of love.

Dreaming

Just dreaming away
The night and the day
When the dreaming is good.
When the dreams are scary
They will make you wary
And you'll wake up before you should.

Some dreams make you worry
So you wish they would hurry
And they would come to an end.
Some dreams are memories
And they are sure to please.
Most of these are of some friend.

If you're being chased
And you're making haste,
It seems like you're going slow.
If you can't find your car
And don't know where you are
And don't know where to go.

You wake up in a sweat
And your clothes are all wet,
Then you find out it's not real.
Those dreams are nerve wracking
For they are distracting,
And that's how they make you feel.

Some dreams make us sad,
Some dreams make us glad,
Some dreams are one of a kind.
Things that we dream
Are not what they seem,
They're just fantasies of the mind.

Our Castle of Dreams

There are many dreams behind locked doors—
Dreams that didn't receive encores.
Some rooms have dreams that have gone astray—
Dreams that will never return this way.

Unfinished dreams are stored away
To be finished another day.
Way down in the cellar below
Is where dreams that cause us stress will go.

In the large rooms we store our mistakes
And from them we learn what it takes.
The empty rooms will be used later
For dreams that could be even greater.

In the rooms way up in the tower
We sit and dream by the hour.
Dreams that we actually believe
That some day somehow we will achieve.

Our lives are built around our dreams.
They show us the way, or so it seems.
When we think of what a dream comprises,
We know why life is full of surprises.

Fulfilling our dreams gives satisfaction
Knowing that it was due to our action.
Dreams are meant to give us direction.
They're not meant to give us perfection.

There are two kinds of dreams, you see.
That is the way it is meant to be.
One dream gives us consternation.
The other gives us motivation.

Shadows on the Wall

Do you remember the shadows on the wall?
We could make them big or we could make them small.
Almost anyone could make the barking dog,
And some were able to make the leaping frog.

The church with its steeple and birds with their wings,
We made bunny rabbits and all sorts of things.
We each took our turn at using the light
To make the shadows that gave us delight.

Then at night after we had all gone to bed
There were these strange creatures up over our head.
There were more of them when we looked toward the wall.
Some seemed to be big and some seemed to be small.

It seemed like they all were moving around,
But the strange part was there was never a sound.
We watched them into the wee hours of night,
Then covered our head and they went out of sight.

Now it was hard for us to go to sleep,
So we decided to try counting sheep.
When we woke up the next morning at dawn,
The shadows had left and they were all gone.

The Dilemma

When your eyes are twitchy
And your nose is itchy
And you've a vase in each hand,
As it is starting to ease
You are wanting to sneeze
And a fly is trying to land.

You try to shoo it off
And then you have to cough
You think what will happen next.
You try to find a place
To set down at least one vase
For now you are really perplexed.

You can't find any space
For you to set down a vase
You wonder what you should do.
The fly is coming back
For another attack
And your nose still itches too.

To top it off now you trip
And both of the vases slip
And they land upon the floor.
Both of the vases shattered
And all of the pieces scattered.
You wonder can there still be more.

The sad part of all this
Is how much you will miss
The vases you've had so long.
But you clean up the mess
And as you do you guess
Nothing more should go wrong.

But that is not your fate
And things don't hesitate
Your troubles still continue
So now it's up to you.
You have to see it through
And give it all that is in you.

The Rabbit and the Hare

I thought I saw a hare but it turned out to be a rabbit.
I thought I would be able to just reach down and
    grab it
But it was so quick and ran so fast that it got away.
There may not be another rabbit come this way today.

Now you tell me a hare and a rabbit are one and
    the same
And it would be all right to call either one by either name.
I thought a rabbit is a member of the hare family
And that it is not as large or as strong as a hare would be.

How did this get started about the rabbit and the hare?
Does it really matter? Does anybody really care?

Fantasies

Little Miss Muffet sat on a tuffet
Eating her curds and whey.
Little Bo Peep has lost her sheep
For they have all gone astray.

Mary had a little lamb
That followed her to school.
What made the little lamb do this?
It was the April fool.

Jackie Horner sat in a corner.
I really don't know where.
But when Mother Hubbard went to her cupboard,
She found that it was bare.

Gather around
Come one come all
To see Humpty Dumpty
Have his great fall.

Why was the Pussy Cat
Put in the well?
Johnnie Green knows,
But says he won't tell.

Why was Mary so contrary?
Wouldn't her garden grow?
The little girl with the little curl,
Is the only one to know.

Why did the mouse run up the clock?
Was it just because of the ride?
Or was it because a thing like this
Had never before been tried?

Where oh where has my little dog gone?
Where oh where did he go?
He's up on the mountain and won't be back
For he is stuck in the snow.

To replace the teeth that you have lost,
Give the tooth fairy a call.
She's the only one that you can see
For she has got them all.

It's almost time for Easter
And the bunny's on its nest.
This is where the eggs come from
Just like you might have guessed.

Little Boy Blue
come blow your horn.
The snowman is waking
As sure as you're born.

The willow is weeping
Because it is sad.
The mocking bird's singing
Because it is glad.

Come Pied Piper
And blow your flute.
The wise old owl
Don't give a hoot.

Four and twenty blackbirds
baked in a pie.
Who's this dainty dish for—
Tommy Tucker and I.

Grandma Moses had a fall
When she went off her rocker.
She didn't watch what she was doing
'Cause she was such a talker.

Yankee Doodle came to town
Riding on his pony.
He went to the nearest store
And bought himself a Sony.

There was an old woman
Who lived in a shoe.
But the Three Blind Mice
Say that is not true.

Twiddle De Dum and Twiddle De Dee
Three men in a tub set out to sea.
Along came a wave and upset the three
And they are about as wet as can be.

The headless horseman
Had no brain,
But then neither
Did Ichabod Crane.

Why did the dish run
Away with the spoon?
They went to visit
The man in the moon.

Simple Simon met a pie man
Going to the fair.
He asked him if he could help
As long as he was there.

The Night They Stole Santa's Sleigh

Santa felt this would be a good flight.
He was leaving earlier that night.
He had this feeling just because
As he waved goodbye to Mrs. Claus.

It was another cool crisp night.
The moon and stars seemed twice as bright.
Santa thought it might happen some day
As he made his rounds the usual way.

He left his sleigh for just a minute.
They stole it with everything in it.
When he returned he saw it was gone.
He had hoped to finish before dawn.

Off in the distance he heard a noise.
The reindeer sleigh and all of the toys
Had crash landed and fell to the ground.
The ones who stole it could not be found.

The toys were scattered all about.
Santa just couldn't figure it out.
Why should someone do this to him?
Perhaps a prankster on a whim.

Some broken antlers and gimpy hoofs
But still able to fly to the roofs.
Santa could make it before daylight.
For Santa it was a frightful night.

Nowheresville

The inhabitants of this make-believe place are not quite the
    same.
Whenever they go out to play, they only have one game.
The losers are the ones who always get three cheers.
The winners are crying banana flavored tears.

When they go to church they only have one pew.
That is where the preacher sits so he is in full view.
The congregation sits up front and they sing the songs.
The choir is any who comes and any who belongs.

The schools operate in a very special way.
The children hold the classes and the teacher has
    no say.
The stores operate on a very different basis.
The keeper memorizes all the people's faces.

He comes to their homes to collect their bill.
He joins them in their dinner and always gets his fill.
This place has no leaders, it's share and share alike.
Those who shirk their duties are told to take a hike.

There are no policemen nor a jail house neither.
The way the system operates, there's no need for either.
The people always go their way and move about freely.
It may seem strange to you but that's the way it is really.

This is the tale of Nowheresville—a place you would like to
    see.
Once you have seen it, it's the place you would like to be.

If

It isn't the who what or why that makes the "diff"
It isn't the when where or how, it's the "if"
If I had been there sooner and hadn't been so late,
If only they hadn't had to stand around and wait.

If things had been different, maybe things would be better.
If maybe I had thought to write you a letter,
If I had the money I could buy me a car.
If I did, I wouldn't have to walk so far.

If it doesn't rain, it will probably snow.
If it does, then tomorrow it will show.
If I could, I probably would.
If I didn't, I probably should.

If I hadn't, I'll wish I had.
If I did, then I'd be glad.
If I can, then I will.
If I can't, it will be there still.

If it was, it wasn't right.
If I had only won the fight.
"If's" go on and on and make most of our decisions.
"If's" will also have a part in making our revisions.

About the Author . . .

A relatively new author, in terms of experience and recognition, Charles Clifford Myers, youngest of six children, was born in 1908 in Blairsville, Pennsylvania, raised in Nebraska, then spent most of his married life in California.

His formal education, two and one-half years of college, majoring in business management, was interrupted by the great depression.

His occupations include substitute mail carrier for four years; variety store fifteen years, five years as manager; musician during depression six years; Douglas Aircraft Company thirty years; retired in 1972.

After his wife passed away, he lived with his son in Denver, Colorado, for a couple of years. In 1981 he moved to Fowlerville, Michigan, where he now resides.

His desire to pass information of their families on to their children inspired him to research and write their family history, and his autobiography.

This was the beginning of a new hobby, which evolved into writing various articles. He wrote his first poem in 1985, which he found to be an enjoyable method for expressing his thoughts and feelings.